BLOOMING
With
JESUS

*Turning Everyday
Idioms into
Daily Devotions*

KIMBERLY HUFF JOHNSON

XULON PRESS

Xulon Press
2301 Lucien Way #415
Maitland, FL 32751
407.339.4217
www.xulonpress.com

© 2022 by Kimberly Huff Johnson

All rights reserved solely by the author. The author guarantees all contents are original and do not infringe upon the legal rights of any other person or work. No part of this book may be reproduced in any form without the permission of the author.

Due to the changing nature of the Internet, if there are any web addresses, links, or URLs included in this manuscript, these may have been altered and may no longer be accessible. The views and opinions shared in this book belong solely to the author and do not necessarily reflect those of the publisher. The publisher therefore disclaims responsibility for the views or opinions expressed within the work.

Unless otherwise indicated, Scripture quotations taken from the Holy Bible, New International Version (NIV). Copyright © 1973, 1978, 1984, 2011 by Biblica, Inc.™. Used by permission. All rights reserved.

Scripture quotations taken from the New King James Version (NKJV). Copyright © 1982 by Thomas Nelson, Inc. Used by permission. All rights reserved.

Scripture quotations taken from the King James Version (KJV) – *public domain*.

Paperback ISBN-13: 978-1-66286-179-6
Ebook ISBN-13: 978-1-66286-180-2

This book is dedicated with love and a grateful heart to my wonderful husband, Hil Johnson. You have encouraged and supported me to complete this project and I thank the Lord for your unconditional love every day.

You truly live the example of Ephesians 5:25, "Husbands, love your wives, just as Christ loved the church and gave himself up for her".

"When you pass through the waters, I will be with you; and when you pass through the rivers, they will not sweep over you."

Isaiah 43:2a

IN UNCHARTED WATERS

In uncharted waters means you're in an unfamiliar circumstance because you have no previous experience to help you figure it out. This comes from using a nautical chart showing the depth of the water, hazards, and tides to help navigate safely through the coastal waters.

My grandma was very influential in my life and growing up I got to spend the night with her a lot. I remember her always saying these funny random things which made no sense at the time.

Now that I'm an adult, I too say these random idioms which seem to pop into my mind out of nowhere. Over the course of time, my children said I needed to write these things down and reveal what they actually mean. The more I wrote down, the more I remembered and then I began to investigate where they originated from.

During the incubation period of the pandemic, to find comfort and solace, I started writing from my heart and the Lord inspired me to turn these everyday idioms into daily devotions.

To say I am *in uncharted waters* is an understatement, but as I navigate through this process, I'm reminded again and again the Lord is with me and I'm following His will. I want everything I do to glorify God and if one thing I've written brings someone into a relationship with Jesus, I want Him to say to me as it says in Matthew 25:21, "Well done, good and faithful servant."

As you read through these devotions, I hope you find these writings inspirational when you see how the Lord has connected the dots between the idioms, the Scriptures, and my life experiences. He is ever present in our lives and longs for us all to continually grow into a deeper and deeper relationship with Him.

I have no idea where this journey will take me, but I do know God is drawing me closer and closer to Him each day through revelation and insight He gives me through His Word.

"A greedy man stirs up dissension, but he who trusts in the Lord will prosper."

Proverbs 28:25

A BIRD IN THE HAND IS WORTH TWO IN THE BUSH

A bird in the hand is worth two in the bush is an old proverbial saying meaning to be content with what you have, rather than risk losing it all. This idiom dates back to Medieval times when falconry was popular for hunting and the bird being held provided numerous meals whereas a bird in a bush would only provide one meal.

None of us have to look very far to see the greed taking over in our world today. It seems we live in a disposable society. Back in the day when something broke, whether it was a shoe or the washing machine, it was repaired. Now it's tossed out and replaced with something bigger and better.

In the teachings of Jesus, money and greed were talked about a lot. Greed can destroy us and in fact it is one of the seven deadly sins. When we allow the accumulation of wealth to become our motivation, we lose our focus on God and never find contentment. We must be careful not to drift away from godly teachings and fall into the trap of greedy desires which can consume us.

Jesus tells the parable of the rich man with such an abundant harvest he tore down his existing barns to build larger ones. He was so focused on what he had, he lost sight of what was important and in the end he died. We're not supposed to store up things on this earth but store up treasures in heaven. We do this by helping others in their time of need.

Jesus also warned us saying in Luke 12:15, "Watch out! Be on your guard against all kinds of greed; a man's life does not consist in the abundance of his possessions." So, we need to remember a *bird in the hand is worth two in the bush* and share with others what we have.

"If the Lord delights in a man's way, he makes his steps firm;"

Psalm 37:23

A STEP IN THE RIGHT DIRECTION

A step in the right direction is an old idiom meaning progress is being made in someone's personal growth or advancing a project successfully. This alludes to moving forward when walking.

It's not always easy to know which direction you should go, especially if the path you choose means changing the course you're comfortable with. God has a way to nudge us and make us uncomfortable where we are, so we know in our hearts it's time to make a change. Stepping out in faith takes courage and trust.

Growing up, I went to the same church all my life because that's where my grandparents went. Just as I went to the same dentist because changing was never even a consideration, I belonged there.

Years ago, we were uprooted from the church we attended because of the decisions made by some members. We knew immediately the Lord was nudging us to leave. Changing churches is hard because you've invested time, fostered relationships, and are comfortable there. But growth doesn't happen until you make a move and take that first step out of your comfort zone.

We found a new church where the love of Christ is projected, a servant's heart is groomed, and where God's Word is taught. A church where God is worshiped, and the presence of our Lord can be felt through the embracing arms of its members. We knew the moment we walked through those doors years ago we had found a new church home.

Peter spelled it out pretty clearly for believers in 1 Peter 2:21, "To this you were called, because Christ suffered for you, leaving you an example, that you should follow in his steps." When we follow Jesus, our steps will always be in the right direction.

"Nor should there be obscenity, foolish talk or coarse joking, which are out of place, but rather thanksgiving."

Ephesians 5:4

A WET BLANKET

If someone is being referred to as *a wet blanket*, the person is dampening the fun of others usually because they disapprove of the activity. Back in the day, a wet blanket was kept in the kitchen to quickly smother a fire, so you see where the analogy came from.

When our youngest daughter was in nursing school she told me about one of the classes she was taking. I forget the exact name, but it was about gender and feminism. I'm thinking to myself, "What in the world are they teaching you?" As she delved into the study, it was about acceptance, compassion, and fairness. This class was to inform the students about real stereotypes and injustices occurring on a daily basis.

In one of her assignments, she had to read a book and it talked about becoming a wet blanket or a party pooper. For instance, when you're hanging out with your friends and if someone makes an insensitive remark or a negative comment about someone, it's your job to say something. Be sensitive to the feelings of others.

Ephesians 4:29 says, "Do not let any unwholesome talk come out of your mouths, but only what is helpful for building others up according to their needs, that it may benefit those who listen." We all want to have a good time when we're with our friends, but Scripture speaks harshly about those who don't control their tongues and have fun at the expense of others.

There are several verses which talk about people who mock others, one of which is Proverbs 17:5, "He who mocks the poor shows contempt for their Maker; whoever gloats over disaster will not go unpunished." As believers we're called to be a *wet blanket*, to stand up for what is right, support each other, and love unconditionally ... just as Jesus would do.

"So we fix our eyes not on what is seen, but on what is unseen. For what is seen is temporary, but what is unseen is eternal."

2 Corinthians 4:18

STUCK IN A RUT

If someone says they are *stuck in a rut*, they feel like life has become mundane, repetitive, boring, or nonproductive. It's difficult to make progress because of the lack of ambition, loss of zeal, or sometimes it's just fear holding someone back. This alludes to the days of the horse drawn carriage where the wheel would get stuck in a rut in the road.

When we were first married, we lived in an older house which needed some love, so we put our blood, sweat, and tears into it to make it our home. We painted, refinished the floors, and even knocked down a wall. I remember meticulously painting the old wooden pane window in the bathroom and I was so proud of the job I had done. Except I forgot one little thing, I didn't move the sash up and down after I painted so the paint that had dripped into the ruts dried, locking the window in place.

I've felt like that old window at times in my life… stuck. Not feeling productive, accomplished, or even valued. Was I really doing what the Lord wanted me to do? Was I living my best life in every aspect and giving it my all? Being a stay-at-home-mom, by the world's standards, I found it hard sometimes to find my worth. My sole job was raising children, being a devoted wife, and managing the household, but was it enough?

I think we all feel *stuck in a rut* from time to time but when we put our focus back on the Lord, we become content again and He moves us forward. God will renew our strength and encourage us just like Philippians 4:19 promises, "And my God will meet all your needs according to his glorious riches in Christ Jesus." He has a plan and a purpose for each of us, and who would have ever thought, oh so many years ago I would be writing devotions today.

"Whoever believes in me, as the Scripture has said, streams of living water will flow from within him."

John 7:38

GO WITH THE FLOW

Go with the flow usually describes the person who is easy to get along with, compromising, and doesn't cause conflict so they follow the majority. This has been around for centuries with the analogy to the natural flow of water.

We like to go kayaking on the New River because we can put our kayaks in and drift with the current for hours with little effort while enjoying beautiful scenery along the way. But if we were to put them in and paddle against the current, it would be a very strenuous workout.

When I've reflected on my life in the past, I know God was giving me subtle nudges to bring me closer to him. Before I was a believer, I drifted through life without any regard as to what His plans were for me, just like I let the current take me while I was on the river. Once I accepted Jesus, I let God become my guide to get me through the waters of life.

There are several passages in the Bible referring to Jesus as being the living water. Water which is not stagnant but vibrant and producing life. Jesus says in John 4:14, "but whoever drinks the water I give him will never thirst. Indeed, the water I give him will become in him a spring of water welling up to eternal life." Jesus wants us to have a vivacious abundant life.

When we choose to make living for the Lord our priority, our entire attitude changes. We just begin to see things in a different light. Things that once seemed important no longer matter. We acquire a gentler spirit, being less combative and easy going. 1 Thessalonians 3:12 says, "May the Lord make your love increase and overflow for each other and for everyone else, just as ours does for you."

The Father filled us with the Holy Spirit the day we accepted Jesus enabling us to love the unlovable. As we fill up on the living waters of Jesus, His love can't help but overflow to others and make us a kinder, more gentle soul. As believers, we tend to *go with the flow* rather than create arguments or discord among others.

"Let us throw off everything that hinders and the sin that so easily entangles,"

Hebrews 12:1a

THROWING IN THE TOWEL

Throwing in the towel is said when someone quits doing something because they cannot succeed. This originates from boxing because a towel is thrown into the ring to signal the end of the fight.

Once I took a pottery class and it was intimidating. I thought it would be easy, but you have to apply the exact amount of pressure on the clay in order for it to form an attractive object. As you throw the clay on the wheel, you use your hands to form this lump of mud into a vessel by pulling upwards while the wheel is spinning.

As I was learning this craft, I couldn't help but think about how we're compared to clay in the Bible. Isaiah 64:8 says, "Yet, O Lord, you are our Father. We are the clay; you are the potter; we are all the work of your hand." There is a beautiful hymn, "Have Thine Own Way Lord" written by Adelaide Addison, which was inspired from this verse. She writes, "Have Thine own way; Thou art the potter, I am the clay. Mold me and make me after thy will...".

Sometimes we all feel defeated and lose hope, feeling like a glob of clay on a wheel that keeps spinning in circles. I know I have. But during these times it's important to remember we're all a work in progress. We are a work of His hands and He is literally molding us into His likeness just as I was molding the clay into a vase.

Apart from God we're nothing but a shapeless mound of mud but God molds us into something useful and beautiful. So, no matter how tough our day may seem, don't *throw in the towel* because God's still working on us, and He has us in the palms of His mighty hands.

"and the one the Lord loves rests between his shoulders."

Deuteronomy 33:12b

GOT A CHIP ON YOUR SHOULDER

I grew up hearing the idiom *got a chip on your shoulder,* so I've always known it meant someone has an unpleasant attitude, caused by resentment, anger, or jealousy. When I looked up where this came from, it actually was from someone placing a wood chip on their shoulders and daring someone to knock it off, wanting to instigate a fight.

I have been around someone before and all they seemed to do was complain. She reminded me of the insect in the book, "The Grouchy Ladybug" by Eric Carle. This is a great book about a ladybug of course, who is never satisfied and flits from place to place always ready to pick a fight. My friend, like the ladybug, made it her objective not to get along with anyone and created discord.

The Israelites also had an attitude problem because rather than having a grateful heart for being freed from the bondage of Pharaoh, they complained to Moses and Aaron. Because of their disgruntled attitude they had to wander around in the desert for forty years. If their attitude would've been more agreeable and obedient, they probably wouldn't have had to wander so long.

As I've gotten older, I realize I don't have to stay in the company of a person with *a chip on their shoulder.* I want to be in the presence of a person who is full of joy and enjoys life rather than looking for something to grumble about. 2 Timothy 2:24 says, "And the Lord's servant must not quarrel; instead, he must be kind to everyone, able to teach, not resentful." As Christ-followers, we're to cultivate a heart full of gratitude and contentment so we'll be a light in this dark world. Our disposition reflects what's in our heart.

Philippians 2:14, "Do everything without complaining or arguing," God is telling us not to have a grumbling spirit because everything we do is to bring honor to Him. When we're in Christ, we're able to guard our hearts, endure the hard things with grace, and give Him the glory every step of the way.

> "Let us acknowledge the Lord; let us press on to acknowledge him."
>
> Hosea 6:3

PRESS FORWARD

Press forward means to continue to make progress in a forward motion even when faced with obstacles or difficulties. This comes from Philippians 3:14 when Paul speaks of pressing on towards a goal.

It seems life gets in the way of our progress sometimes and for every step forward, we're taking two steps back. It's easy to feel overwhelmed when there are deadlines, demanding children, friends in need, mounting laundry and the list goes on and on.

In the hustle and bustle of completing our tasks it's so easy to forget why we do what we do. We are both physically and emotionally drained by the end of the day, and we haven't squeezed any time in there for God.

Paul reminds us there is an ultimate prize waiting for us at the finish line, an everlasting glory. Philippians 3:14 says, "I press on toward the goal to win the prize for which God has called me heavenward in Christ Jesus." Even he, who walked with Jesus, had to continue to remind himself that he had to press on.

We serve a loving powerful Lord. A God that cradles us in the palms of His hands when we are discouraged. Our God is able to equip us to multitask when we think we have nothing left to give, and gives us endurance to achieve more than we are capable of.

We have to replenish our soul by spending time with the Lord and *press forward* to the reward He has waiting for us. I never realized how important spending time in His word was until I started doing it. I have been in countless Bible studies with ladies who devoted time to the Lord daily so I would commit to doing it myself but not follow through. Spending quiet time with the Lord has brought me into a deeper understanding of just how much He cares for every aspect of our life.

"And we know that in all things God works for the good of those who love him, who have been called according to his purpose."

Romans 8:28

THERE'S MORE THAN ONE WAY TO SKIN A CAT

To say *there's more than one way to skin a cat* is a humorous way to remind someone there's more than one way of doing something to reach the same goal. I don't think cats were actually ever skinned; however, they are the subject of many idioms.

Now that my husband has retired, he has taken over the cooking, reorganized the spices and rearranged the refrigerator. I'm grateful he loves doing it; however, this has been an adjustment for me. Through this process I have realized how rigid I had become. I did things my way and that's how I liked it but God has taught me humility and grace.

I remember years ago I watched a cooking show, and they showed the easiest way to dice an onion. When I was with my mom, I showed her what I had learned and rather than thanking me, she got upset and said, "I've got sense enough to cut an onion".

The older we get, the more set in our ways we become, but we shouldn't be like that. I like to be right, but I realize how wrong I am about so many things. I believe we're never too old to learn something new and grow in knowledge.

As believers, the longer we're in fellowship with the Lord, the deeper our relationship with Him becomes. Our trust grows stronger, our reliance on Him becomes more frequent, and our love for others becomes deeper. As our journey with God continues, we become a gentler spirit, I know I have. We are no longer concerned about small things but strive to be open minded. Just because we're used to doing something one way does not mean it's the only way because *there's more than one way to skin a cat.*

"Do not curse the deaf or put a stumbling block in front of the blind, but fear your God. I am the Lord."

Leviticus 19:14

A STUMBLING BLOCK

A stumbling block is an idiom used in the Bible on several accounts. It means an obstacle which stops the progress being made or a belief keeping someone from having a relationship with God.

We love to hike, but as we go on these trails, we really have to watch where we step and be aware of the roots and rocks which can make us fall. Erosion will cause rocks to jut out making the path treacherous in places causing us to trip.

Paul says in 1 Corinthians 8:9, "Be careful, however, that the exercise of your freedom does not become a stumbling block to the weak." In this chapter, he is talking about whether it's okay or not to eat the leftover meat from a sacrifice. Some Christians believed it was a pagan act, but the mature believer knew this had no effect on their salvation. Just like having to watch our step when we are hiking, Paul is reminding us to be aware of others around us so we don't cause them to misstep and lose their faith.

God wants to make sure we're not the reason someone rejects Him. We're all on our own growing curve in our relationship with the Lord but we're called to be a living example to the new believer, so we don't deter them in their walk. The last thing we want to be is an obstacle keeping someone from having a relationship with the Lord.

In the Lord's Prayer it states in Matthew 6:12, "Forgive us our debts, as we also have forgiven our debtors." The word debts here means the same as sin. It infers sin causes us to fall away from our walk with God. We are all going to stumble, that's a fact but we don't have to stay down. The good news is our false steps are forgiven the day we accept Jesus as our Lord and Savior. So, in our journey to grow closer to Jesus, we need to be mindful and make sure we're not ever *a stumbling block* to others.

"If you do not stand firm in your faith, you will not stand at all."

Isaiah 7:9 b

A FIRM BELIEVER

To be *a firm believer,* one has to have a solid dedicated conviction on what they believe and cannot be swayed or yield to peer pressure.

Owning a house is a wonderful blessing but with that comes the responsibility to continually maintain it. Our front steps are brick and over time the mortar has deteriorated causing a hazard. As we took the bricks apart, we realized the steps were placed directly on the ground so as the soil settled, the mortar crumbled.

Before we could redo the steps, my husband had to pour a concrete foundation. When we're finally ready to lay the bricks, we have to get the mortar to be the exact consistency. We're not brick masons so YouTube was invaluable. If the mortar was not firm enough the bricks would shift and become unstable.

Aren't we a lot like those steps? Without having a firm foundation on what we believe, we crumble in our convictions and can be swayed to believe in untruths. I believe that's why there are so many different religions with so many doctrines. Christianity is the only religion having a living Savior who has risen from the dead.

God has given us sound doctrine to guide us and teach us through the Scriptures. We need to know what the Word says so we can stand firm against the false teachings. Many times, the Scriptures are twisted to suit the world's lifestyle so we have to make sure what is spoken is truth.

Throughout the Bible the phrase "stand firm" is used to illustrate the posture we are to have when we believe in Christ. We have the power to stand against all the forces of evil and tribulations coming our way. 2 Corinthians 1:21-22 says, "Now it is God that makes both us and you stand firm in Christ. He anointed us, set his seal of ownership on us, and put his Spirit in our hearts as a deposit, guaranteeing what is to come."

"Surely the nations are like a drop in a bucket;"
                                                Isaiah 40:15a

A DROP IN THE BUCKET

A drop in a bucket is an insignificant amount when compared to something else. This comes from Isaiah where God's greatness is being compared to great nations where there is no comparison.

I think it's actually impossible for our human minds to comprehend the true greatness of God, He just created us that way. His powers are boundless, He is omnipresent, and He knows our thoughts before we can even articulate them.

As I study God's Word and learn more about His attributes, I can't help but become overwhelmed as I realize how much He loves us. We're all made in His likeness, and with that being said, you would think we would all want to act more like Him, being gracious, kind, loving, gentle, and have compassion.

When the problems in our society seem to spiral in a downward motion, I can physically feel myself becoming more and more anxious.

I have to stop myself from worrying and consciously remember God is in control. He calms my spirit and soothes my soul because He has compassion on His children.

When our focus remains on God, the worries of the world fade because the injustices happening are just *a drop in a bucket* compared to how BIG our God is. Fear and faith cannot occupy the same space, so I choose the latter. I can sleep at night because I put my trust in Him and He gives me peace that wipes away all anxiety.

> *"For you know that it was not with perishable things such as silver or gold that you were redeemed from the empty way of life handed down to you from your forefathers,"*
>
> 1 Peter 1:18

RUNNING ON EMPTY

Running on empty means you continue to work and do what you have to do although you have no energy. This originates from continuing to drive a vehicle while the fuel indicator is on "E".

Life happens and we get busier and busier. Our day is filled with appointments, chores, phone calls, practice schedules and a host of other must-to-do things on our list. How often do we ever put on the list "spend time with God"?

I remember years ago we had a speaker at church who showed this beautiful illustration of why we need to make God the top priority in our daily lives. He had this large glass cylinder surrounded by rocks of all sizes. One by one he would add a rock and name an activity associated with it. He started with smaller stones and said they were chores and progressively kept adding the rocks. When he got to the largest rock which represented God, it wouldn't fit. But when he reversed the order and placed the rock of "God" first, all the other rocks fit perfectly into the container.

God wants to be the top priority in our life rather than us just squeezing Him in. He wants us to fill up on His Word daily so we can combat the evil forces around us. Just as our body needs food for energy, our spirit needs feeding too. Paul reminds us the Holy Spirit dwelling in us enables Christ to live in our hearts and says in Ephesians 3:19, "and to know this love that surpasses knowledge–that you may be filled to the measure of all the fullness of God."

He is ready, willing, and able to "fill us up" with His perfect love so we don't have to be *running on empty*. All we have to do is ask.

"Everyone was amazed and gave praise to God."

Luke 5:26

YOU COULD HAVE KNOCKED ME OVER WITH A FEATHER

Whenever someone uses the idiom, *you could have knocked me over with a feather*, they're saying they are so surprised or astonished at what they have just seen or heard it has left them in shock.

Last year I had been praying specifically for a situation laying on my heart. In my small mind I had it all figured out how God would answer my prayer. But in one simple phone call, it was revealed the situation no longer existed! Gone! Vanished! All the what-ifs and the worst-case scenarios had disappeared.

One of my favorite verses is Mark 11:24, "Therefore I tell you, whatever you ask for in prayer, believe that you have received it, and it will be yours." What an awesome promise. I claim that promise. Our God is so wonderful He answers prayers beyond our comprehension.

In John 11:1-44, we learn of the story of Lazarus, Mary and Martha's brother. As they send word to ask Jesus for help, He comes but it's in His timing, not theirs. By the time Jesus arrives, Lazarus is dead along with all of their hope. But Jesus reminds them to keep their faith and even though the body had already started to decay, Lazarus was brought back to life. Can you imagine what it must have been like trying to comprehend what they just witnessed. I cannot! They must have all stood there in awe when Lazarus walked out of that tomb.

As we pray for different concerns entering our life, we can never forget God will answer if we believe. It may not be the answer we want or when we want, but He will answer. When we give it all to the Lord in prayer, sometimes the answer will *knock us over with a feather.*

> *"Therefore put on the full armor of God, so that when the day of evil comes, you may be able to stand your ground,"*
>
> Ephesians 6:13

STAND YOUR GROUND

Stand your ground means you stick to your convictions, your beliefs, and refuse to change your opinion. It can mean you defend yourself when attacked. This idiom comes from Ephesians 6 where Paul is reminding the followers of Christ to stand firm in their beliefs so they can withstand spiritual attacks.

I found it interesting that in many states they actually have a stand-your-ground law in their books which means a person has the right to use deadly force to defend themselves against a crime.

Most of us have been spared from having to defend ourselves from a physical attack but if we're honest, most of us have been attacked on what we believe, I know I have. As believers, we have to stand on our biblical principles and not be swayed to believe the untruths the secular world throws at us. The waters are becoming more and more murky as to what the truth really is.

We don't have to look too far to see how hard the evil one is working. There's division among us on issues that shouldn't matter which cause friction in families and workplaces. That's why there are so many different churches of the same denominations in the same area, a disagreement occurred which couldn't be reconciled so they split and formed another church.

James 4:7 spells it out pretty clearly, "Submit yourselves, then, to God. Resist the devil, and he will flee from you." I just love the visual of the devil fleeing. You see, when we're walking close to God, we have the power to stand up for what is right with boldness.

We all must *stand our ground* now more than ever, but we can't stand firm if we're not standing on solid ground. When Christ alone is the foundation of our lives, we become unsinkable.

"Be perfect, therefore, as your heavenly Father is perfect."

Matthew 5:48

THE HEIGHT OF AMBITION

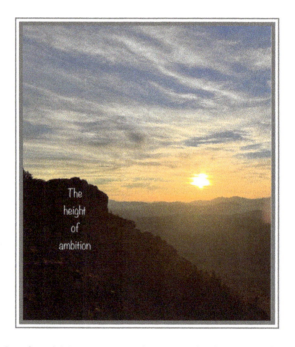

The height of ambition means to have reached your goals; you have set the standard of excellence. This can also be used as a sarcastic remark towards someone being lazy.

Once we had kids of our own, the question was always where did they want to go to college rather than if they wanted to go. We didn't care if they went to a four-year college or trade school, but we wanted them to have a goal. We believed a child strives to meet the bar of achievement set before them, so we set the bar high.

None of us are perfect! There was only one perfect person who ever walked on this earth in human form, and He was crucified on a cross. Jesus set the bar for perfection. He was kind, generous, forgiving, and I could go on and on. Just as we are to be role models to our children, Jesus was the role model for us. Even though we can never attain a perfect life, we can strive for perfection when we follow the example God gave us in Jesus. We desire to achieve the standards God has set before us because of the power of the Holy Spirit living in us.

I am task driven. When I have a project, it motivates me to imagine what the end product will look like. If it's furniture I'm working on, I try to envision where the completed piece will go in my house.

The same principle can be applied in our daily lives. What is the end goal? What is my purpose? The word goal is defined as the object of someone's ambition, the target, or end result. We are to strive to achieve the heavenly goal given to us as believers. Paul reminds us to keep pressing towards the goal of completion which is ultimately living a life illuminating the love of Jesus. Just as the winner of a competition wins the prize, the Christian wins the ultimate prize which is eternal life; *the height of ambition.*

"I am the true vine, and my Father is the gardener."

John 15:1

WITHER ON THE VINE

To say something is going to *wither on the vine,* infers something will not be productive. This comes from the appearance of grapes that haven't been picked when ripe, but instead they dry up on the vine.

Vineyards fascinate me and I love to see fields with rows and rows of perfectly lined vines. Grape vines grow quickly and produce many shoots which weave and wrap around anything they can find to cling to, so to maximize the quantity of grapes a vineyard produces, the vines are trellised and carefully pruned.

Jesus tells us we also have to be pruned to maximize the fruit we produce. I love it when Jesus uses word pictures to illustrate the message He was teaching. In John 15:1-8, He compares us to the branches on a grapevine. He reminds us in John 15:5, "I am the vine; you are the branches. If a man remains in me and I in him, he will bear much fruit; apart from me you can do nothing."

The fruit Jesus is referring to are the godly virtues we receive when we accept Jesus as our Lord and Savior. He yearns for us to grow in our knowledge and continue to thirst for the living water, a thirst only His Word can quench. John 15:6 warns, "If anyone does not remain in me, he is like a branch that is thrown away and withers; such branches are picked up, thrown into the fire and burned." We are fruitless apart from our union and fellowship with Christ. Just as the branch has no life when it is severed from the vine, we are lifeless when we are not living for the Lord.

When we study God's Word, pray, and have fellowship with other believers, we're nurturing a relationship with Christ. The closer we draw to the Lord, the stronger our desire to please Him becomes. God loves us and has called us to love others and not *wither on the vine.*

"Cleanse me with hyssop, and I will be clean; wash me, and I will be whiter than snow."

Psalm 51:7

PUT THROUGH THE WRINGER

For anyone to have been *put through the wringer,* they have experienced or are going through a very difficult trial in their life. This idiom originates from the old washing machines that used wringers to squeeze the water out of wet laundry.

Life just isn't fair. I know this to be true and sometimes there is no rhyme nor reason why certain things happen the way they do. One minute we're just living our life, doing the best we can, then out of nowhere we've been blindsided, ... we've been put in totally different circumstances.

Sometimes we have no control over awful things that happen in our lives and then other times the wounds are self-inflicted, which is the case for David. David acknowledges he had allowed himself to fall into temptation, lusting for Bathsheba and then navigating the death of her husband to cover his tracks. He felt so filthy he pleaded for God to make him clean again by washing away his sin. David asks to be cleaned with hyssop, which is a flowering shrub in the mint family used for ceremonial cleansing. He knew if God washed his sin away, his severed relationship he once had with the Lord would be restored.

Most of us feel like we have been *put through the wringer* at times. I know I have. We will never admit we enjoy the process of being tested, but when we get to the other side we have been transformed, whether here or in heaven. Just as the wringer squeezes out the excess water in our laundry, the trial we have just endured refines us. We are a little more Christlike because we have felt the presence of the goodness and grace of God. Even though we suffer when we're going through these trials, God promises to restore us.

"But our citizenship is in heaven. And we eagerly await a Savior from there, the Lord Jesus Christ,"

Philippians 3:20

A WATCHED POT NEVER BOILS

A watched pot never boils is an old expression simply implying time seems to stand still when you're waiting for something to happen. This idiom obviously stems from the patience needed when bringing water to a boil.

I can remember there used to be a ketchup commercial showing someone holding the bottle upside down. The ketchup was so thick, it flowed at a snail's pace causing all this anticipation to build up. They actually played the song for dramatic effect. The point they were making was that good things are worth waiting for.

We have become an "instant" society. We order our stuff and it is "primed" to our house and if we don't know the answer to anything we just plug it into our phones or computers and "bam", the answer appears on the screen. In fact, our ketchup bottles are now squeezable, so we don't even have to wait on the ketchup.

To wait on something causes a yearning and a desire. As a parent we want to give our children the best life possible but when they want every new toy, we really should be careful and not overindulge them. There's a sense of pride and ownership when we have to work for what we want because it builds our character.

As a believer, we eagerly await the returning of Christ. While we're here, we try to live a life bringing honor to God because we know this life is temporary. Although Christians are fully involved in the world and interact within it, we're not of it, we're like aliens because we don't belong here. None of us know when Jesus will return, but we know He will in His perfect timing. We just have to wait and remain diligent. As we wait for something to happen, our excitement builds but we must remain patient.

"Let your conversation be always full of grace, seasoned with salt, so that you may know how to answer everyone."
                                                            Colossians 4:6

SALT OF THE EARTH

When a person is said to be the *salt of the earth,* it means they are honest, genuine, and have good strong morals. This idiom comes straight from Matthew 5:13, "You are the salt of the earth. But if the salt loses its saltiness, how can it be made salty again? It is no longer good for anything, except to be thrown out and trampled by men."

This verse is part of the Sermon on the Mount Jesus delivered by the Sea of Galilee. Salt is a preservative and an additive to foods to enhance the flavor and in this passage, Jesus is comparing the Christian to salt. He is telling us we have to be bold in our faith, so we'll stand out in the world.

When we stand up for what is right and make our voices heard, we may not realize it, but others take notice. When they see Christlike qualities in us; they may ask, "What is different about that person?" We may never know the impact we have on others. We're called to stand out, stand up, and stand firm in His Word.

When I was a young mama, I was invited to join a ladies Bible study. I learned so much from these women but mostly I learned about God's grace. It didn't take me long to know these ladies were who they proclaimed to be. They were followers of Christ and it showed up in their words, tone, and actions.

Our desire should be to live a life of humility like *the salt of the earth.* It's easy to react to the negative behaviors of those around us but we're called to be set apart. We should try to show extra kindness to everyone, especially the people we encounter who don't seem nice. Who knows, we may be the only "Bible" they see.

"I will instruct you and teach you in the way you should go; I will counsel you and watch over you."

Psalm 32:8

OFF THE BEATEN PATH

Off the beaten path means to venture into unfamiliar territory or take a route that's less traveled. A path becomes beaten down when it's frequently used.

Let's face it, most of us like doing things our own way. We go through our day and thoughtlessly choose the direction we should go and then when it doesn't work out the way we thought, then we pray for guidance from God.

I love to go hiking, and living in the mountains of southwest Virginia, there are countless trails to scenic mountain top overlooks or breathtaking waterfalls. But before I set out on one of these trails I need to know where I'm going and make sure I stay on the right trail. I also need to know the distance and the degree of difficulty so I can be prepared.

I was taught at a young age that I was in control of my destiny. The choices I made were right for me without any consideration of what plans God had for my life. Often the choices I made were not the right ones, but I can look back and see how He continued to steer me in the direction I should go. He redirected my steps.

We can think we're in control but ultimately, it's God who's in control of our lives. He continues to watch over us even when we get *off the beaten path* and have walked away from Him. He desires for us to seek biblical wisdom so we know with confidence the direction in which we should go.

Now that I'm a believer, I do try to seek God's will for my life. My heart's desire as I mature is to grow in an authentic relationship with the Lord. Being a hiker, I especially love the promise in Psalm 18:36, "You broaden the path beneath me, so that my ankles do not turn," This is such a beautiful image of how God specifically makes the path He desires for us to take both wide and clear, so we'll be on steady ground.

> *"Do not be like the horse or the mule, which have no understanding but must be controlled by bit and bridle or they will not come to you."*
>
> Psalm 32:9

CHOMPING AT THE BIT

Chomping at the bit means you're impatient to start something but you're being restrained from engaging because of circumstances you have no control over. This comes from the action from horses when they champ at the bits in their mouth. Although chomping is the word commonly used in this idiom, "champing" is the actual word.

The older I get the more patient I've become although I still catch myself blowing it at times. I remember how frustrating it was trying to get to church on time with little kids, rushing out the door only to realize one didn't have their shoes on. Once they were found, my child had to exhibit their independence by tying their own shoes. I can remember telling myself, "Just breathe".

I love the patience exhibited by the prodigal son's father. The man must have been heartbroken when his son requested his inheritance and even more disappointed when he found out it was all wasted away. But yet when the son returned home, the father ran out to meet his son, hugged and kissed him.

God has the same kind of patience with us. Even when we go astray, our Father is waiting with open arms to greet and embrace us when we return to Him. This story gives us a beautiful visual of how full God's heart becomes when we repent of our sinful lifestyle and turn our hearts back to Him. He waits patiently on us to reciprocate the love He has for us.

We're all guilty of *chomping at the bit* from time to time but we have to remain patient because sometimes life's not on our timetable. Waiting creates a yearning and a spiritual growth happens when our desire is to please Him. Jesus intercedes on our behalf and the Spirit sustains us. As we grow more patient with the Lord, we in turn exhibit more patience with others.

> *"He said to them, Go into all the world and preach the good news to all creation."*
>
> Mark 16:15

ONLY SCRATCHING THE SURFACE

Only scratching the surface means to deal with only the superficial part of something while there's much more to be done. There are several theories as to where this originated from, but some believe it comes from agriculture. The soil has to be properly prepared for planting rather than just scratching the surface.

I love the heart of the missionaries. They have empathy for others in need and selfishly leave all the comforts of home and go! That's what God has asked each of us to do so we can share with others the undeniable love of Jesus. We don't have to go far because our own neighborhood is a mission field.

Our youth group goes to Mexico every other year to build houses and I had the privilege of going with my daughter several years ago. We built simple wooden structures on a concrete slab without running water but for someone with nothing the house was perfect. It was such a beautiful experience to witness the grateful hearts for what they had just received.

These teenagers were more than willing to give up a week in their summer and serve the Lord. To Go! Love! Do! They showed families that spoke another language the love of God without speaking a word, by literally becoming the hands and feet of Jesus.

There are people all around us hurting. Maybe they need financial help or just a shoulder to cry on but we can actively make a difference in their lives when we engage. When an opportunity presents itself, we have to have a willing spirit and put our faith into action. As believers, we have an obligation to show, share, and reflect the love of Jesus to everyone around us because we have only begun to *scratch the surface*.

> *"my son, do not go along with them, do not set foot on their paths;"*
>
> Proverbs 1:15

RUN OF THE MILL

The idiom *run of the mill* means to be average, nothing spectacular or of outstanding quality. This originates from goods being manufactured in a mill that have not been inspected for quality so they haven't been graded.

My grandparents were both weavers for Burlington Mills. They moved around a lot and typically lived in a cookie-cutter mill village house. There was nothing average about Grandma, she was a hard worker and prided herself on being one of the top weavers because of the first quality cloth she produced.

As we grow in our relationship with Jesus, we're being conformed daily into the likeness of Christ. 1 Peter 2:9 says, "But you are a chosen people, a royal priesthood, a holy nation, a people belonging to God, that you may declare the praises of him who called you out of darkness into his wonderful light." We are now the recipients of God's great mercy and grace.

I think most of us want to be good at something, or at least we should. I know I have the gift of hospitality. I go out of my way to make sure when anyone stays in our home, they're well fed and comfortable because I'm glad they made the journey to see me.

As believers, aren't we supposed to greet everyone with that same enthusiasm? There was a slogan going around some years ago, "What would Jesus do?" There were bracelets, T-shirts, and even bumper stickers but when out in the world it's hard to find Jesus living in the hearts of others sometimes. We get so caught up in doing what we need to do, as fast as we possibly can, we forget to be kind to those around us.

I don't want to be another *run of the mill* person on the street because we can all make a difference with just on person at a time. You never know what seeds are being planted.

"He will be like a tree planted by the water that sends out its roots by the stream."
                                                    Jeremiah 17:8a

THE ROOT OF THE MATTER

The root of the matter means to get down to the essential part of something so we can understand the reason behind what is happening or why we are doing it. This idiom actually derives from Job 19:28, "How we will hound him, since the root of the trouble lies in him,".

I have been in Bible studies ever since I became a Christian because it not only helps me understand God's Word, but it also cultivates fellowship among believers. We just wrapped up a study in our church called "Rooted" which was deep, but also just got down to the simple truths of the Scriptures. This book challenged me to step out of my comfort zone and put myself "out there" like no other study I've ever been in. Our pastor summed it up pretty well in three little words. KNOW, GROW, and GO.

As believers we're to dig deep into the Scriptures so they can be ingrained in us. When we know what the Word says we begin to grow in our relationship not only with God but also with others. Once we have this knowledge we're called to go and share this wonderful news. It reminds me of the children's song which talks about letting our lights shine.

We have the opportunity to make a difference in the world one small step at a time. When we thrive, those around us hopefully see something different in us. The language we use, the reactions we make, and the actions we take are being motivated by the Holy Spirit living in us.

For any plant to grow it must have an ample root system. Once a food source is established it begins to flourish and produce a bud which soon emerges into a bloom. Just as the flowers attract bees to pollinate and feed, we attract others to Him when we live a life that's pleasing to the Lord. *The root of the matter* is simple, when we are rooted in God's Word we will grow and bear fruit.

"Praise the Lord, O my soul, and forget not all his benefits—"

Psalm 103:2

COUNT YOUR BLESSINGS

When someone says to you, "You better *count your blessings*", they're saying you should be grateful rather than complaining because the situation could be a lot worse.

When I was little, there were several dinners fixed that were less than desirable. Mama would make oyster stew, fried liver with onions, salmon cakes ... you get the picture. I was required to try it, but I never acquired a taste for any of it. All I ever heard was, "Well you better be thankful you've got something to eat, there are starving children all over the world!"

We tried to instill in our children to have a thankful heart also and not take things for granted. I wanted them to realize life can be hard at times, but through those rough patches there's an opportunity for our faith to grow.

Most of us are blessed beyond measure and I think it's important to remember to thank God for all we have. Even during the most difficult times in our lives, we can feel the presence of the Lord because His grace will carry and guide us.

When we actually praise God out loud in front of others, we are witnessing without even realizing it. We're acknowledging how great and wonderful our Heavenly Father is because we know all we have comes from Him.

God's blessings are all around us, we just have to take the time and notice. My youngest daughter and I love to chase sunsets so we try to reach the optimal view before the sun sets behind a ridge. Each one is uniquely different and beautiful. Grandma always said it was God's painting at the end of the day displaying His spendor.

Sometimes at the end of the day I have trouble falling asleep so I will *count my blessings* as I drift off to sleep. God wants us to continually give Him praise because He is worthy. When He is the source of our joy and our focus is on His goodness, the worries of the day cannot distract us. Whatever the day brings may we continually see the blessings coming from our Heavenly Father who loves us.

"Give thanks to the God in heaven. His love endures forever."

Psalm 136:26

LOVE YOU A BUSHEL AND A PECK

A bushel and a peck are dry measurements particularly used by farmers. There are four pecks to a bushel basket, with each peck equaling eight quarts. When someone says, "*I love you a bushel and a peck*", they're saying they love you a lot.

In the summertime I remember we would all pile in the back of the truck, (Daddy would put the tailgate up because we were going on the highway ... safety first) and go down to the peach orchid to get a bushel of peaches. When we got home, Mama would start washing, peeling, and slicing the peaches because she canned everything, but she would save a bowl for later.

After supper we would get out the rock salt and the old hand cranked churn to start the process of making homemade ice cream. We would all have to take turns churning the peachy concoction which seemed like it took forever but it was so worth it. Daddy didn't use words to let us know we were loved but we knew it through his actions.

Throughout Scripture, God reminds us of His abundant love for us. I've always told my kids love is an action word. You can say you love someone, but when you show it, they know it. Jesus was the living example of how we're to treat others. He constantly showed love to everyone around Him and went out of His way to meet the needs of those who called on Him. He fed them, healed them, listened to them, helped them and prayed for them. He has called us to do the same.

God demonstrated sacrificial love for us when He sent His only Son to perish for our sins. A love which we as humans can't comprehend. Our guest preacher made a powerful statement which really resonated with me. He said we became a living sacrifice to God when we accepted Jesus as our Lord and Savior. With that being said, unlike the days of the animal sacrifices, because we are alive, we can crawl off the altar. The visual of us crawling away really made me stop and think. We do have a choice because God gave us "free will". We have to choose to stay in the presence of the Lord but our willingness to be obedient is a testament to our devotion to God.

It's easy to love those who *love us a bushel and a peck* but our heart's desire should be more Christlike so we can show love to everyone. God wants us to impact others through sacrificially serving those around us because we are the church.

"The blessing of the Lord brings wealth, and he adds no trouble to it."

Proverbs 10:22

MORE TO DO THAN YOU CAN SHAKE A STICK AT

To say you have *more to do than you can shake a stick at,* means something is so numerous you can't count whatever you're referring to. Some believe this originated from shepherds because they used a staff to herd their sheep.

Grandma said this all the time, especially on Saturdays before she had the family over for Sunday dinner. Between the cleaning, prepping the food, and cooking, she was very busy. I can now relate when I'm preparing for my own children and their families to come for a visit. There's a lot to do!

In 1 Kings 18, we learn of the story about Elijah testing Baal. During this time, there was a great famine in the land and Jezebel was killing all the prophets of Israel. Elijah summoned over four hundred prophets of Baal to Mount Carmel to basically have a show down to see which God was real and who could actually send fire to ignite the fire for the burnt offering.

After the alter was prepared, the Baal worshippers began praying for fire to be sent. Elijah began to taunt them by saying maybe their God was too busy to answer their prayers because no fire ever came. When it was Elijah's turn, he had the alter drenched in water not once but three times.

Elijah prayed to the Lord that His power would be known among the people so they would again turn their hearts back towards Him. God answered his prayer by sending fire which consumed everything in sight at the alter, including the standing water and the stones.

God is never too busy for us. He hears all our prayers and answers us in His perfect timing. Even though we may have *more to do than we can shake a stick at,* we can know with confidence God knows our heart and hears our concerns.

> *"Carrying his own cross, he went out to the place of the Skull (which in Aramaic is called Golgotha)."*
>
> John 19:17

A CROSS TO BEAR

If someone says they have *a cross to bear*, they are dealing with a difficult situation or having to endure a burden. This idiom comes from the fact Jesus actually had to carry a cross to his execution site. Crucifixion was commonly used as a scare tactic to visualize what happened to criminals during the Roman Empire.

Our youth pastor gave a beautiful analogy about the shape of the cross. The cross is constructed by two beams, one vertical and the other horizontal. The vertical beam signifies the relationship Jesus has with His Father while the horizontal beam symbolizes the love Jesus has for us. The image of His arms spread open for us to come to Him. He endured humiliation, ridicule, flogging, and an unfathomable death on a cross... all for us.

The cross has become a fashion statement to wear around our necks, but do we really stop and reflect about what those crosses stand for? The cross stands for an incomparable and sacrificial love, it represents belonging to the kingdom of heaven. Crosses are empty because Jesus is no longer there, He rose from the dead and now sits on the right side of God.

When Jesus was collecting the twelve men to serve on His ministry team, He used the cross to emphasize the total commitment to Him. Upon accepting the position, it meant devotion even to the point of death. Matthew 16:24 says, "Jesus turned and said to his disciples, If anyone would come after me, he must deny himself and take up his cross and follow me."

When we are burdened with something we just need to remember to go to our Heavenly Father in prayer. Regardless of the cross we're asked to bear, it's possible to withstand anything because we have the Holy Spirit to empower us.

"neither height nor depth, nor anything else in all creation, will be able to separate us from the love of God that is in Christ Jesus our Lord."

Romans 8:39

ALL OVER CREATION

The idiom *all over creation* is used to exaggerate how extensively someone has searched for something or someone.

It's difficult to lose someone and not have a clue as to what happened to them. When Grandma was young, she had a brother who just vanished into thin air, he simply disappeared. There were no Amber Alerts back in the day and even though they searched and searched, they never found a trace of him. She always wondered what happened, but she never gave up hope that maybe one day he would walk through her door.

There are many unexplained mysteries in this world we will never understand. We can look all over creation to find answers and although we may never know, God does. He knows the answers before we even have the question because He's omnipotent. This concept is hard for us as humans to even wrap our heads around, but we can take comfort in knowing our God is bigger than anything we will ever have to face.

There is one thing we can know with confidence and it's the God of the universe loves us and longs for us to believe in Him. The day we accept Jesus as our Lord and Savior, the Holy Spirit begins to reside in us and gives us a desire to be more like Him.

Keeping our faith during the good times is easy but in the valleys of our life we sometimes forget to look up. The Lord is refining us during those trials, but He will never leave us there. We are much more appreciative of the view from the top of the mountain when we look to the valley from which we ascended.

> "A fool finds no pleasure in understanding but delights in airing his own opinions."
>
> Proverbs 18:2

DON'T AIR YOUR DIRTY LAUNDRY

When someone reveals an unflattering story about themselves or shares details too personal, another person might tell them not to *air their dirty laundry*. Today it's more commonly known as TMI or too much information.

None of us have to look very hard to find someone sharing something on social media which would be better left "unshared". Just keep those embarrassing photos or thoughts to yourself.

Most of us have done something we're not necessarily proud of but despite our faults, God loves us anyway. For some of us it's hard to let go of our past. It's like a weight around our necks weighing us down, that is if we let it.

The good news is regardless of what our past looks like, we're forgiven when we confess those sins to God. I was in a study group once where we did this exercise to illustrate just how God sees our sins. We all had to write something down weighing heavy on our hearts and then we wadded the paper up and threw it in the fire.

The moment we accepted Jesus into our hearts, (quicker than the flames consumed the paper), our past transgressions were forgiven and gone forever. We no longer have to drag our past into our future because we're free from the bondage of our sins.

Luke 7:36-50 tells a beautiful story about a woman who was bold enough to approach Jesus in a Pharisees house. While she wept at the feet of Jesus, she washed them with her tears, dried them with her hair and then poured perfume on them. Jesus knew she was burdened by her sinful life so He forgave and told her that her faith had saved her, now she could go in peace. She was so ashamed of her sins, she felt she was only worthy of washing His feet.

I've made mistakes but through my imperfections, I have grown spiritually. I really try to make each day pleasing to the Lord and I don't *air my dirty laundry...* that's between me and God.

"In the same way, count yourselves dead to sin but alive to God in Christ Jesus."

Romans 6:11

DEAD AS A DOORNAIL

When you say something is as *dead as a doornail* it's basically useless. This comes from the fact an actual doornail is an ornamental stud on a door for decorative purposes only. Mama always said this about a dead plant.

When I was growing up, we went to church on Sunday, unless we were sick. God was woven into the foundation of how we were raised but there was not a living relationship with Jesus.

I have heard people say they don't go to church because it's just full of hypocrites and "they're no better than the rest of us". That is a true statement but church is like a hospital for the sinner, we all need to go to become better. Jesus says in Mark 2:17, "It is not the healthy who need a doctor, but the sick. I have not come to call the righteous, but sinners." We all fall short of perfection. There was only one perfect person who walked this earth and we hung Him on a cross.

The moment sin entered that garden we became alienated from God, so now we have to fight against the darkness of the world. We have to cultivate a relationship with God to bring us back into a loving fellowship and we do this by spending time reading His Word and prayer. Our spiritual health depends on it and is determined by the amount of time we do this.

The good news is God's love for us was so great He sent His Son to restore our communion with Him. He longs for us to accept Jesus as our Lord and Savior so we can re-establish a relationship. Through grace, we are no longer *dead as a doornail* because we have been redeemed and the Holy Spirit lives in us. Now we have the incentive to share the love of Jesus by loving and serving others.

> *"Therefore show these men the proof of your love and the reason for our pride in you, so that the churches can see it."*
>
> 2 Corinthians 8:24

THE PROOF IS IN THE PUDDING

The proof of the pudding is in the eating is the original old English expression meaning you had to taste something to know if it was good or not. Today it has been shortened to *the proof is in the pudding* and it simply means the end result will prove what you say.

To prove something is to test it and evaluate its worth. In our society we seem to be busy comparing ourselves to someone else so we can be the best mom ever, post the most perfect picture, volunteer the most, be the hardest worker, and be the perfect wife.

I had a girlfriend who was divorced, and she was constantly reinventing new and improved activities for her kids because she said she wanted her children to want to be with her more than their dad. The pressure she put on herself was exhausting and needless because her love for her children was more than adequate.

We don't need to fall into the trap that our works validate us. Yes, we do all these things because of the love we have for our families but we don't have to kill ourselves proving it. All we need to give is unconditional love just as Christ gives unconditional love to us. We should always examine our hearts and make sure our intentions are pure and honor God.

We don't have to prove our worth to anyone. We are favored children of God, we are His masterpiece, His handiwork, and we're fearfully and wonderfully made. Our faith is more precious than gold and *the proof is in the pudding* when we put our hope and trust in the Lord because our actions will speak louder than words.

*"Therefore, if anyone is in Christ, he is a new creation;
the old has gone, the new has come!"*

2 Corinthians 5:17

A NEW LEASE ON LIFE

A new lease on life means someone is energized because they have been given a fresh start to improve their life after going through hardship. This originally refers to someone who has recovered from a grave illness.

Living in the mountains of southwest Virginia, our winters can be harsh. The naked trees make the season gloomy and spring can't get here soon enough. As the earth finally awakes from a deep sleep, new life begins to pop out everywhere.

One of my favorite flowering trees is the Redbud. Mama always called it a "Judas" tree and I never gave it much thought until I looked it up. Legend has it the tree stood tall and had white flowers until Judas hung himself from a branch. Afterward the tree never grew straight again, and the blooms became reddish/purple. They're the first trees that "pop" from winter's sleep to remind us of the forty days of Lent. As the blooms subside and fade away, perfectly heart shaped leaves begin to emerge from the tips of every branch to remind us of God's love.

I don't know if the legend is fact or fiction but it is a neat story and a visual reminder of just how much Jesus loves us. God reveals Himself to us constantly through His creation.

We all have a chance for *a new lease on life* when we make the decision to live a life for Christ. Romans 6:6 says, "For we know that our old self was crucified with him so that the body of sin might be done away with, that we should no longer be slaves to sin–". Our old self fades away and we begin to emerge as a new creation transforming into the likeness of Christ just as the blooms on that tree grow into leaves.

> *"Leave them; they are blind guides. If a blind man leads a blind man, both will fall into a pit."*
>
> Matthew 15:14

BLIND LEADING THE BLIND

The idiom *the blind leading the blind* comes straight from the Bible. In Matthew 15, Jesus is using the parable to illustrate the hypocrisy coming from the Jewish leaders. The teachings being taught were rules and regulations made by man and were leading the people astray.

Growing up I can always remember our family taking a vacation. Usually, it was a week at the beach but this one particular year my parents thought it would be a good idea to visit the battlefields of Virginia, Luray Caverns and then ending up at Kings Dominion. As kids, all we could think about was getting to the amusement park because in our opinion, if you've seen one battlefield you've seen them all.

Upon leaving the third battlefield, Daddy got turned around and couldn't find the road he needed. This was before GPS and apparently Mama, the map reader, dropped the ball. Finally, after hearing the pleas from the backseat, he pulls into a country store to ask for directions.

Daddy gets back into the car and is relieved that one of the men in the store lived right down from the very road we were looking for so all we had to do was follow him. The man gets into his blue pickup and we fall in behind him. Now this guy starts driving faster and faster like he's trying to lose us. Finally, he slows down and turns into his driveway... we followed the wrong blue pickup.

It's easy to get lost when you don't know who you're following. I mean really know them. Jesus tells us to follow Him because we will never be led astray. In John 9:39, "Jesus said, For judgment I have come into this world, so that the blind will see and those who see will become blind." We no longer have to remain like the blind leading the blind because now we can see.

"Repent, then, and turn to God, so that your sins may be wiped out, that times of refreshing may come from the Lord,"

Acts 3:19

BARKING UP THE WRONG TREE

When someone is *barking up the wrong tree,* they have the wrong idea about something or have jumped to the wrong conclusion. This originates from an animal being hunted and it gives the dogs the slip by pretending to climb one tree while escaping to another.

It's very difficult to clear your name when you have been wrongly accused, especially if the person has made up their mind that you're guilty. This happened to me over a group message with some girlfriends while planning a trip. Texts were flying back and forth as we were trying to finalize the arrangements and one friend assumed something which was never said.

We all make mistakes because none of us are perfect. We're going to mess up but when we do, we need to swallow our pride, admit we're wrong, and learn from our blunder. 1 John 1:8 says, "If we claim to be without sin, we deceive ourselves and the truth is not in us." I love how my Bible has study notes to detail the meaning of the Scriptures, however with this passage no explanation is given because no additional explanation is needed. Plain and simple ... we all sin!

As believers we have to guard ourselves not to cast judgment on others and keep a forgiving spirit. *Barking up the wrong tree* leads to false accusations, hurt feelings, and broken relationships.

We are called to forgive others just as Jesus did and allow the Holy Spirit dwelling inside us to help. When we do this, all broken relationships can be repaired. Just as rain washes the dust off plants and gives nature a fresh clean start, God refreshes our spirits and our sins are wiped away ... forever.

"We live by faith, not by sight."

2 Corinthians 5:7

HINDSIGHT IS 20/20

We always have a better perspective when we reflect and analyze past experiences, we've been through so it's a very common thing to say *hindsight is 20/20.* This comes from the fact 20/20 is perfect vision and hindsight is looking backwards.

When we're in the midst of a difficult period in our life sometimes it's hard to see the grace of God. We don't see how we're shielded and protected until we're on the other side and reflect. When I look back on some difficult seasons from my past, I see so much clearer the goodness of God and how I was carried through the storm.

Even though the disciples were with Jesus through His entire ministry and witnessed the miracles that occurred, they really didn't comprehend who He was until after His death. Oh, they knew Jesus was the son of God, but I don't think any of them thought He would be killed; much less rise from the tomb. John 12:16 says, "At first his disciples did not understand all this. Only after Jesus was glorified did they realize that these things had been written about him and that they had done these things to him." John says this after he witnessed Jesus making his way into Jerusalem on the back of a donkey with an explosive crowd waving palm branches.

Retrospectively John wrote this book to document what he had seen and lived over the past years. It was only after the resurrection of Jesus the believers were given the Holy Spirit to give them spiritual knowledge. They gained insight when they reflected back on what had happened as they walked with Jesus, saw the miracles, and heard Him speak.

Although *hindsight is 20/20,* we have the Holy Spirit to guide us and give us clarity. When we seek God's will in our life, we will feel His presence even when we're in the midst of those dark patches. The Holy Spirit gives us peace, joy, and a calmness which can only come from God.

"Plans fail for lack of counsel, but with many advisers they succeed."

Proverbs 15:22

FLYING BY THE SEAT OF YOUR PANTS

Flying by the seat of your pants means something is done by instincts rather than following directions or using mechanical aids. This is an old aviation phrase used when the pilot flies using their own judgment rather than the navigational equipment in the plane.

When our youngest was three, she got a cozy coupe for Christmas which said, "some assembly required". After the kids were finally asleep, the assembly process began without reading the directions first. Let's just say there is a particular order in which things had to go on and at one point a rubber mallet was involved. Miraculously the coupe made it under the tree intact.

Isn't that our nature? We think we know how to do something, so we *fly by the seat of our pants* rather than following directions or asking for help. I think that's how it was with many of us before we became believers. We just did life our way. God has a plan for each of us and has a way to instruct us in the way we should go and even redirect our steps sometimes by placing roadblocks in our paths.

I can't help but think of the life of Paul before he became a follower of Christ. He was literally stopped in his tracks on his way to persecute more Christians. God used the very man who despised Him to bring others to Him. After his conversion, Paul waited three years before he started his ministry. He's informing us where his knowledge came from saying in Galatians 1:12, "I did not receive it from any man, nor was I taught it; rather, I received it by revelation from Jesus Christ."

Not all of us had a "Damascus Road experience", sometimes God softens our hearts gradually drawing us closer to Him. Regardless of how we got here, He's given us all a conscience to guide us.

> *"You need to persevere so that when you have done the will of God, you will receive what he has promised."*
>
> Hebrews 10:36

HANGING ON BY A THREAD

To be *hanging on by a thread* is admitting you are barely getting by. The overwhelming sensation of defeat or being in a precarious situation. This idiom originates from when Damocles, a courtier of ancient Syracuse, was given a banquet by King Dionysius. The king was so annoyed with Damocles, he had a sword suspended by a single hair over where Damocles was seated.

Sometimes I try to solve a problem myself, become defeated, and then I turn to God. I need to turn to God first and seek His guidance. When I do this, my fear dissipates, I remain calm, and I know regardless of the outcome, God's got this because He's ultimately in control.

We all know the story of Hagar who was sent away with Ishmael. Hagar was abandoned, lost, starving, parched, without hope, and had nowhere to go. Out of desperation she put her dying son under a bush and left him there so she would not be able to watch him die. When the Lord heard the cries of Ishmael, they were both saved and told not to be afraid because he would be made a great nation.

I can't help but wonder if Hagar would've been spared a lot of heartache if she had cried to the Lord when she first got sent into the desert. She should have sought the guidance and protection from God rather than trying to make it on her own.

I'm like Hagar sometimes, I think, "I've got this!", and I take matters into my own hands and attempt to figure things out on my own. God desires for us is to seek Him first and ask for His help, guidance, and wisdom before we get into a dire situation.

Seeking godly wisdom restores our peace when we feel we're only *hanging on by a thread*. This wisdom is not only factual information but also an insightful spiritual application in our life.

"The fear of the Lord is the beginning of knowledge,"

Proverbs 1:7

TO THE BEST OF MY KNOWLEDGE

When someone uses the phrase, *to the best of my knowledge,* they're speaking the truth about a topic to the best of their ability.

Knowledge is powerful. Regardless of our background or economic status we're given a mind equipped to learn. The beautiful thing about living in this country is you can grow up and be anything you want when you put your mind to it.

But sometimes knowledge makes people too powerful. They get puffed up and start saying things they think are true rather than sticking to the facts. A prime example of this was displayed during the recent pandemic. Officials would release information one day and contradict themselves a week later, the inconsistency was frustrating.

There is one source that is reliable, steadfast, and it never contradicts itself. The Bible! This book is full of truths, guidance and wisdom for us to follow to live our best life.

Before I became a believer, I would sometimes read the Bible but there were many things that didn't make sense and I just didn't understand. The more I read, the more I began to develop a hunger to read God's Word. 1 Corinthians 2:14 explains, "The man without the Spirit does not accept the things that come from the Spirit of God, for they are foolishness to him, and he cannot understand them, because they are spiritually discerned."

Now when I read the Scriptures, they are more than merely words written in a book, they are the living and breathing Word of God speaking to my heart. The Scriptures are the perfect Words of God, expressing just how deeply our Heavenly Father loves us. They are truths penetrating our hearts, chastising our thoughts, and directing our paths. The Bible is a wonderful source of information and when our facts come from the Scriptures, they really are *to the best of our knowledge.*

"All men will hate you because of me, but he who stands firm to the end will be saved."

Matthew 10:22

STICK OUT LIKE A SORE THUMB

To stick out like a sore thumb means to be very noticeable, not blending in and different. This obviously comes from the fact that when we have an injured thumb, it is noticeably hurt, and we attempt to protect it. My fingers will crack in the winter and will become very sore. When this happens, I inevitably seem to hit that finger and re-injure it.

When I was in school, I tried to blend in because I didn't want to be different from the other kids. I remember begging Mama to buy me a pair of Levi's because that's what everyone was wearing. They were the first pair of pants I ever owned without elastic in the waistband. I was so proud.

Now as a believer, I realize we're called to stand out and not follow the crowd. Romans 12:2 says, "Do not conform any longer to the pattern of the world, but be transformed by the renewing of your mind. Then you will be able to test and approve what God's will is—his good, pleasing, and perfect will." God wants us to be set apart.

I love to sew but in order for the pieces to fit perfectly together, I must follow the pattern exactly. Paul is telling us not to follow the pattern of the world but for us to follow the perfect pattern of Jesus. Because of the power of the Holy Spirit dwelling in us, we are transitioning into the likeness of Christ. When we seek the will of God, we will have both spiritual and moral growth.

In the crazy world we're living in right now, it's a good thing to *stick out like a sore thumb.* We are called to be bold in our faith and to stand up for what is right. It takes courage sometimes to do this but we are empowered by the Holy Spirit to stand with confidence.

"There is a time for everything, and a season for every activity under heaven:"... "a time to weep and a time to laugh, a time to mourn and a time to dance,"

Ecclesiastes 3:1,4

HAVE A BALL

When someone tells you to *have a ball,* they're telling you to have a good time at whatever you are doing. This alludes to the formal dances, or "Balls" which were fashionable in British high society. Debutante balls became quite popular with the upper crust where they would formally introduce their daughters into society in the hopes they would marry into families at the same financial status.

Not everyone likes to dance, but in most cultures, dancing is an expression of celebration and joy. Most of the weddings we have attended have a reception which includes a dance floor.

There are some religious beliefs where dancing is forbidden, but dancing and enjoying life is mentioned in the Scriptures. Especially in Psalms, musical instruments like tambourines and harps are used to praise God. We're to have a contagious joy which spreads to others.

Our perspective about life will either attract people or repel them. When we keep a positive attitude throughout the many different facets of our life, our joy becomes contagious.

Ecclesiastes 8:15 says, "So I commend the enjoyment of life, because nothing is better for a man under the sun than to eat and drink and be glad. Then joy will accompany him in his work all the days of life God has given him under the sun."

Sometimes things get hard and rob us of our happiness, but our joy can never be taken away when Jesus is the source. Life is short so we need to *have a ball* and enjoy every single minute we have on this earth.

"He has made everything beautiful in his time."

Ecclesiastes 3:11a

BEAUTY IS IN THE EYES OF THE BEHOLDER

Beauty is in the eye of the beholder is an old proverbial phrase meaning beauty is subjective. What I may see as beautiful, others may not.

Every mother believes their baby is beautiful. I know I thought each one of my babies were the most beautiful things I'd ever seen. I couldn't help but see the miracle of life that could've only come from God.

God reveals himself in many ways; through His Word, through His creation, and through other believers, just to name a few. When we look at the splendor of His creation, it's mind-blowing to see the intricate details of the bumblebee, the magnificent colors of a sunset, or the brilliance of a butterfly. Our human minds can't comprehend the magnificence of God, we just weren't created that way.

I forget to see God's beauty all around me when I focus on what's happening in the world. My hope is restored when I remember God is still in control and then my fears dissipate. God frees us from all the fear of the unknown when it seeps into our mind and robs our joy.

Many of the Psalms were written by David where he pours out his soul to God in hopes to rekindle the relationship he allowed sin to sever. When we come to the Lord in humility, he is able to redeem us because we are all beautiful in the eyes of our Heavenly Father.

"A stingy man is eager to get rich and is unaware that poverty awaits him."
　　　　　　　　　　　　　　　　　　Proverbs 28:22

TIGHT AS A TICK

The old Southern idiom *tight as a tick* has several meanings. It can mean someone is uncomfortably full after eating a huge meal or someone is extremely stingy with their money. Grandma always said it after eating. Some believe this alludes to the insect which becomes engorged on the blood of an animal. Another theory is back in the day, beds had a mattress, also known as a "tick" which sat on ropes that periodically were tightened to ensure a goodnight's sleep.

Money is always a touchy subject, especially when the preacher starts asking for more from the pulpit. You can physically see people start to fidget in the pew. I think it's just God stepping on toes.

God has called us to be generous with what we have been given. I remember once when we lived in Cheraw, our church was planting another church so they asked us to pledge what we would give in the upcoming year. I thought, "no big deal". But our pastor explained exactly what he meant. He was asking us to promise to give more than what we were capable of and in doing so we would be relying on God to provide through us. The concept was foreign to me but what I witnessed in our small congregation was astounding. The amount raised was above and beyond what our goal was.

In Luke chapter 12, Jesus tells the parable of the wealthy farmer with an abundant crop. Rather than sharing his abundance, he hoards it and even builds bigger barns. This story reminds us to store our treasure in heaven and not on earth.

Most of us have been blessed beyond measure because we have an abundance of food, clean water and shelter. The moral of the story is we're to be cheerful givers, not takers. I can still hear Grandma drilling that in my head when I didn't want to share my stuff.

> *"but those who hope in the Lord will renew their strength. They will soar on wings like eagles;"*
>
> Isaiah 40:31a

SPREAD YOUR WINGS

Spreading your wings means to seek independence from your parents or experience new activities for the first time. This probably originated from the comparison with birds who actually have to spread their wings to leave the nest.

The first time we leave home and actually live away from the protection of our parents can be scary. Some leave and never look back while others have a difficult time adjusting. But one thing is for certain, we'll never know how far we can soar if we don't ever try.

A bird exhibits a great deal of courage the first time they leave the nest. Most infant animals are born on the ground and they gradually get their legs stable before they start walking. Birds on the other hand must literally take a leap of faith out of the nest and trust they will take flight and not plummet to the earth.

Isaiah 40:31 says, "but those who hope in the Lord will renew their strength. They will soar on the wings like eagles; they will run and not grow weary, they will walk and not be faint." There is a really neat explanation about this verse, the word renew, means "exchange". So, when we put our hope and trust in the Lord, He exchanges our fear into strength. He alone equips us to conquer what we set out to accomplish by giving us endurance so we are able to stay strong.

There are many uncertainties in this life, but we can trust beyond a shadow of doubt when we do *spread our wings,* we will soar when we put our trust in the Lord. This is where we put our hope, our strength, and our courage because we know nothing is impossible with God.

"for everyone born of God overcomes the world. This is the victory that overcomes the world, even our faith."

1 John 5:4

THE SWEET SMELL OF VICTORY

The sweet smell of victory is used when you get that euphoric feeling of success. There is probably one thing the human race can agree on, we all like to win. Whether it's an argument, a game, or an election, we all like to be victorious.

It seems in this day and age; people have a hard time accepting a loss. We see it time and time again when the opponent loses in a trial, an election, or a sporting event; protests begin which sometimes lead to violence. We all have to learn to be a gracious loser rather than a sore one because everybody's got to lose sometime.

I remember as a kid singing the popular hymn "Victory in Jesus", written by Eugene Bartlett in church with Grandma. This man had a stroke at the age of fifty-four which left him partially paralyzed and during this difficult time in his life he wrote these amazing lyrics. There is only one victory that matters, and it's the acceptance of our Lord and Savior into our hearts.

Upon our death we will no longer have hope or faith, they will cease to exist because what we have hoped for will be revealed. It's only love which will remain and we will eternally be in the presence of God. While on this earth it is our faith motivating us to follow the commands of God.

As believers we have victory over death. It was sin that brought us under the power of death but through the blood of Christ, we are saved and we're on the winning team for eternity.

As long as we're in these earthly bodies, we will battle our sinful nature and as believers we're called to push daily to become more Christlike. One day we will know the ultimate *sweet smell of victory* when we are in heaven.

"Love your neighbor as yourself."

Mark 12:31

THE BOTTOM LINE

The bottom line refers to the most important outcome to a situation, the end result, or the main point. This phrase is used in corporate America showing the loss or profit margins of their company.

When I tell a story, I go into detail about different aspects that sometimes have no importance to the plot then somehow, I eventually weave back to the topic I started with. I wish I was a little more like my husband because when he tells a story he is able to stick to the topic and gets straight to the point.

During the years of Jesus's ministry, parables were used with each one having a main point. He stayed on topic and taught consistently. Jesus told a word picture making the stories relatable to the culture of the day and they still ring true today.

Word spread fast of His teachings and especially towards the end of His ministry, the religious leaders would try to trap Jesus with His own words. The Jewish rabbis were bound by countless laws so they asked Jesus to reveal the most important commandment. Jesus answered in Mark 12:30-31, "Love the Lord your God with all your heart and with all your soul and with all your mind and with all your strength. The second is this: Love your neighbor as yourself. There is no commandment greater than these." The leaders were so confined by the law, the simplistic answer Jesus gave them was hard for them to comprehend.

We are to love as Jesus loves us; unconditionally, unquestionably, and unequivocally! When we love like this, we are a reflection of Jesus, so in turn others will want to also be a follower.

When I was younger, I would sometimes question my purpose? Am I meeting my potential? What does God want me to do with my life? *The bottom line* is we all have a purpose... to love others and bring glory to God. Period!

"When I said, My foot is slipping, your love, O Lord, supported me."

Psalm 94:18

SLIPPERY SLOPE

To say someone is on *a slippery slope* is to say they are making decisions that are leading them into a disaster. Taking the first step towards the wrong direction can lead to a chain reaction of wrong decisions causing a catastrophic ending.

We love to go hiking and many trails cross creeks. You really have to be careful where you place your foot if you don't want to get wet because the rocks become very slick. Waterfalls are particularly dangerous because so many think they can just walk across the rocks, but this can end very badly.

Life can be like that also. We don't really see the dangers lying beneath the surface until it's too late. We've let temptation lead us astray. David knew firsthand what it felt like to be in trouble and alienated from God. Psalm 40:2 says, "He lifted me out of the slimy pit, out of the mud and mire; he set my feet on a rock and gave me a firm place to stand." When we find ourselves in the depths of despair, the supernatural love of God can give us a foothold on solid ground.

We always need to watch where we place our feet because we don't want to get on *a slippery slope*. God's Word keeps us grounded so we're able to stand firmly against temptations. A foothold is a place where a foot can be lodged, to support a person securely especially while climbing so they won't slip. Just as a climber has to securely plant their foot before taking the next step, as a believer we are securely supported as we climb upward in our relationship with the Lord. When our foothold is embedded in Christ, we're able to discern the difference between the leadership of the Holy Spirit and the deception of the evil one.

> "Your beauty should not come from outward adornment,... Instead, it should be that of your inner self, the unfading beauty of a gentle and quiet spirit, which is of great worth in God's sight."
>
> 1 Peter 3:3-4

BEAUTY IS ONLY SKIN DEEP

The old idiom *beauty is only skin-deep* means even when someone may have a beautiful appearance, their true beauty is reflected in their heart.

Most of us take pride in our appearance and try to put our best foot forward, and this is not an obstacle for a Christian unless it becomes an obsession. God has uniquely made each of us and we are each beautiful in His sight, but what counts is what's in our heart. When we radiate the love of Christ, others see our inner beauty because we're reflecting Him.

In 1 Samuel 16, God sends Samuel to the house of Jesse to anoint a new king of Israel. Eliab was the first son that Samuel met and thought he was the one based on his outward appearance. The Lord said in 1 Samuel 16:7, "Do not consider his appearance or his height, for I have rejected him. The Lord does not look at the things man looks at. Man looks at the outward appearance, but the Lord looks at the heart." While we tend to focus on the exterior looks of someone, God focuses on the character and inner disposition of the person. David, a mere shepherd, was chosen as the king not because of his outstanding stature, but because of the condition of his heart.

As believers we have an obligation to reflect the goodness of Christ in all we do. We need to validate ourselves by our character and not let our appearance define who we are. Our looks will fade but our relationship with Christ will grow and the closer we become to Him, the brighter our light will shine. It's true that *beauty is only skin deep* but when we radiate the love of Christ, we are beautiful inside and out.

"Do not let your hearts be troubled. Trust in God; trust also in me."

John 14:1

ON PINS AND NEEDLES

To say you are *on pins and needles* is saying you're nervous and anxious about an upcoming event. This comes from that uncomfortable sensation you get when recovering from numbness like when your foot "falls asleep".

Oh, I say I don't get anxious but in reality, I do, especially when I'm faced with the unknown. I get anxious waiting for further medical test results because the first one was inconclusive or going on an airplane. I think it's because I don't have control of the situation.

Let's face it, life is full of unexpected issues but I really do try to let go of things I can't control and give them to God. That's all I can do. He truly does give us peace that passes all understanding. A peace which settles our soul and calms our mind. One of my favorite verses is Philippians 4:6, "Do not be anxious about anything, but in everything, by prayer and petition, with thanksgiving, present your requests to God." All we have to so is ask, He's just waiting for us to call on Him.

It's very difficult to be a trusting believer and remain a worry-wart being anxious about everything. God wants us to surrender our concerns and give them to him. He is with us to lighten our load and rid us of any and all anxiety. Being thankful is the antidote to worry. When we focus on what we do have and the blessings before us, the worry about the unknown dissipates.

So, the next time I feel like *I'm on pins and needles*, I need to stop, pray, and let go. When I try to handle the unknowns on my own, I'm becoming arrogant rather than trusting and relying on God. I need to remember worry and prayer are opposing forces for a believer.

"The eyes of the Lord are everywhere, keeping watch on the wicked and the good."

Proverbs 15:3

EYES IN THE BACK OF YOUR HEAD

To have *eyes in the back of your head* means you are very perceptive of what's going on around you and are aware of things happening that cannot be seen.

Respect was not requested from my parents; it was demanded. This was not an option. To honor your mother and father is a commandment, it's number four on the list so it must be pretty important.

As parents we are called to instruct, guide, love and discipline our children. Proverbs 22:6 says, "Train a child in the way he should go, and when he is old he will not turn from it." The word train means to undergo discipline or instruction. Parenting is a huge responsibility which should never be taken lightly. We need to set an example as to how we want our children to behave when they reach adulthood.

There's an old saying, "Do as I say, not as I do", but that's just a poor excuse for bad behavior. We have to set the standard before our children so the lifestyle they mimic is loving, respectful, and obedient. Disciplining children is not the fun part of parenting but it's a requirement. Our job is to nudge them in the right direction so as they grow, the right decisions will become second nature. There are "rules" in society which have to be obeyed or the consequences may be catastrophic, so disciplining our children teaches them to respect authority.

The greatest gift we can give our kids is to be a constant reflection of Jesus and show His unconditional constant love to them daily. We are called to build our children up with encouraging words while steering them in the right direction. Parenting is a huge responsibility, but thankfully we're equipped with *eyes in the back of our heads* to keep them safe and on the right track.

"Come now, let us reason together, says the Lord. Though your sins are like scarlet, they shall be as white as white as snow;"

Isaiah 1:18

AS WHITE AS SNOW

When we refer to anyone or anything being as *white as snow,* we are usually signifying innocence and purity. This comparison is made several times in the Scriptures.

Winter here is usually pretty cold and dreary, filled with sunless skies, brutal winds, and bare gloomy landscapes. Once when my granddaughter was here, she looked out the window and said, "Look Mimmy, it's raining snow."(She's from Florida). As the snow began to accumulate, all the gloom began to fade away. What was left behind was a fresh pure blanket of snow making everything look new.

The change in the landscape reminded me of our lives before and after we came to know Jesus. Sin in our lives separates us from God. We're like the barren trees swaying in the wind, just hoping to survive another day. But the minute we accept Jesus into our heart, He covers us with His blood. God no longer sees our old sinful self but only sees the purity of Jesus. Psalm 51:7 says, "Cleanse me with hyssop, and I will be clean; wash me, and I will be whiter than snow." Hyssop was used in the Old Testament to ceremonially cleanse someone from their sins but once Jesus cleanses us, we're cleansed forever.

I believe God gives each one of us an opportunity to hear the truth and invite Jesus into our hearts but the more we reject Him, the harder our hearts become. God's desire is to bring us back into the fold when we go astray and change our heart of stone into flesh. His handiwork is all around us and I find it difficult not to see the sheer splendor of the works. The beauty of nature alone should open our eyes to our Creator who perfectly designed every detail in spite of our sinful nature.

"Direct my footsteps according to your word; let no sin rule over me."

Psalm 119:133

ONE STEP AT A TIME

When the idiom *one step at a time* is used it means you're taking your time to do something deliberately, cautiously, and gradually. This is an old metaphoric expression comparing life with walking.

When our youngest grandson was just over a year old, he was learning to walk. He was very determined to be steady on his feet before he would be brave enough to let go of what he was leaning on. Only after he felt steady on his feet and had secure balance did he take that first step.

As I watched him struggle to take consecutive steps without falling, I saw the parallel of me constantly trying to live a life which glorifies God. I want to be that determined in my walk and when I stumble, I want Jesus to be the one I lean on to find my balance. I know my sinful nature seeps in when I'm not deliberately focusing on doing what is right, so I have to consciously choose to serve the Lord daily.

We all go through difficult times and so do the ones we love. When they hurt, we hurt too. Sometimes the valleys seem so deep we feel hopeless and we can get lost. Jesus promises He will never leave us there when we seek His face, but the burden is on us to call upon God to guide us out of those valleys. We can know with assurance He will be alongside us every step of the way.

The poem "Footprints in the Sand" is a reflective look at a person's life. Its author, during a dream, is asking God why there is only one set of footprints when they are going through the most difficult times in their life. The Lord's response was, "because that was when I was carrying you".

Life can be overwhelming, especially when we get ahead of ourselves and worry about our future. We just have to breathe and take *one step at a time*. Our steps will always be on solid ground when our trust is placed in the Lord because He gives us guidance, protection, and comfort. He's able to keep us steady on our feet and enable us to live a life glorifying Him.

"Whatever you do, work at it with all your heart, as working for the Lord, not men,"

Colossians 3:23

GET THE LEAD OUT

When you tell anyone to *get the lead out,* you're asking them to get moving, hurry up. Lead is a very heavy metal so figuratively speaking, to remove it would lighten your load making you faster.

When I was in the seventh grade our community participated in a twenty-mile walkathon for multiple sclerosis. The course was woven throughout the town creating this gigantic circle so we would end the walk where we started. I did my due diligence and collected pledges to inspire me to complete the walk.

I remember thinking about mile seventeen I would just perish on the street. My feet began to feel like they weighed a ton and the only reason I pressed on towards the finish line was because of the pledges. My sponsors motivated me because my goal was to give money to the charity, and I didn't want to let them down.

Life is like a walkathon rather than a sprint. We have to pace ourselves and persevere because we know what the ultimate prize will be someday. Our promise of eternal life is the motivation to be Christlike.

We can all be encouraged knowing God is our hope and our strength through those difficult valleys we go through. He invades our spirits through prayer and gives us the power to endure all obstacles. He's waiting for us to seek Him regardless of the situation.

So, in this race we call life, we must push forward with a zealous heart and *get the lead out.* I want to stay motivated to do God's will and not give up regardless of how tired I become. I love the Scripture coming from Philippians 2:3, "Do nothing out of selfish ambition or vain conceit, but in humility consider others better then yourselves." The Lord encourages us to love, revealing a Christlike attitude towards others.

> "You are my refuge and my shield; I have put my hope in your word."
>
> Psalm 119:114

SAFE AND SOUND

Safe and sound is an idiom that's been around for ages. It means to be secure and removed from the threat of any danger. Today it's frequently used in notifying loved ones about safe travels once they've reached their destination.

The other day while my daughter was driving, a rock the size of a baseball slammed into her windshield. The impact shattered the glass but thankfully the safety glass kept her from harm, and by God's grace she was able to stay composed. Hearing her tell the story reminded me of all the times in my life God has protected me from harm, even before I knew Him.

The glass didn't explode because it was designed and constructed for such an impact, to help keep us safe. God protects us the same way because He puts a shield around us just as the windshield did for my daughter. What a beautiful image of the Lord's protective hand around His children sheltering us from harm.

We can take comfort knowing God watches after us. Scripture often refers to God as a fortress which is a fortified stronghold or a person who is not vulnerable to trouble or outside influences. God is our reinforcement against the world, our protector. We can pour out our hearts to Him in good times and difficult times because He will always be with us.

Countless times throughout the Bible, God has intervened to protect His people. In 2 Kings 6, we learn of the prophet Elisha who was being attacked by the Arameans. The king of Aram wanted to take Elisha captive so his army encircled the city, but Elisha could see the greater forces of the heavenly hosts of horses and chariots of fire in the surrounding hills. He prayed the enemy would be struck blind and God answered his prayer, just as He does for us today.

"When pride comes, then comes disgrace, but with humility comes wisdom."

Proverbs 11:2

PROUD AS A PEACOCK

Proud as a peacock means someone is puffed up, full of self-esteem, or strutting their stuff pridefully so to speak. The simile comes from the fact peacocks are known for their spectacular colors displayed on their feathers. The proud male will span his tail to attract a mate.

I'm a proud mama of four wonderful children, and when they soar, my heart does also. They have each set out on their own to spread their wings. Even as they set goals in their lives and reach those accomplishments, I need to remember to stay and humble and praise God for these wonderful children.

In the book of Daniel, King Nebuchadnezzar became so arrogant and proud, he no longer worshiped the Lord. Instead, he had a gold statue erected and ordered the people to bow and worship it because of its great beauty. King Nebuchadnezzar ignored the warnings which were revealed in his dream to repent so the Lord stripped him of everything and banished him into the wilderness.

After living like a wild animal for seven years, the Lord restored his sanity and his nobility because the king humbled himself before the Lord. He says in Daniel 4:37, "Now I, Nebuchadnezzar, praise and exalt and glorify the King of heaven, because everything he does is right and all his ways are just. And those who walk in pride he is able to humble."

So, when we get puffed up and *proud as a peacock* over something we've done, we need to remember to humble ourselves before the Lord so others will see the light of Jesus radiating through us.

"The time has come, he said. The kingdom of God is near. Repent and believe the good news!"

Mark 1:15

IN THE NICK OF TIME

In the nick of time means something is done at the last possible moment and it is almost too late. This derives from when merchants, or scorekeepers used a nick-stick to keep track of points or transactions by putting a notch in a stick.

I am sure we've all had a close call, when something was done, and not a moment too soon. I remember Grandma telling the story about one day while she was busy in the kitchen fixing dinner and all the others were in the back of the house. When all of a sudden, the neighbor busted through the front door, ran to the flaming Christmas tree, and threw it outside. He lived across the road and when he went out to the front porch to have a smoke, he could see flames through the front windows.

They say, "timing is everything" and it sure was that day. Time is something our world revolves around, no pun intended. We wear time on our arms as a fashion statement, we decorate our homes with clocks, and the time is the first thing popping up when we pick up our phones. Our tombstone will even have our time stamp on it.

I know when I pray about something laying heavy on my heart, I want the answer in a timely fashion, but that's not always how God works. God always hears our prayers but it's up to His discretion as to when He will answer.

When the Israelites were making their way to the promised land, food was scarce. As the people began to grumble about their hunger pains, God provided manna from heaven. Each morning when they awoke, the perfect amount was given to them to satisfy their needs for the day. This was a visual reminding us His portion is always enough and He provides more than what is needed.

Our faith grows as we are building our confidence and trust in our Heavenly Father. Just as the Israelites had to totally rely on God's provision to survive, we can trust God will provide for us what we need when we need it, *just in the nick of time.* He hears our prayers and knows our hearts but we'll receive the answers in His perfect timing.

"May your unfailing love rest upon us, O Lord, even as we put our hope in you."

Psalm 33:22

EVERY CLOUD HAS A SILVER LINING

Every cloud has a silver lining is an old proverb said to encourage someone going through a difficult situation, meaning something good can come out of every unpleasant circumstance.

Grandma and I would lay on a cot on the back porch and hunt for objects in the clouds as they moved across the sky. We could both look at the same cloud and she would see one thing and I would see something entirely different, we each had our own perspective.

It's sometimes difficult to keep a positive outlook when we're in the midst of a difficult situation. We find ourselves going down the rabbit hole of fear as everything around us begins to crumble.

That's when we have to stop ourselves and remember God is still in control. Throughout history there have been some pretty dark times, but through it all, the human spirit has prevailed. James 1:12 says, "Blessed is the man who perseveres under trial, because when he has stood the test, he will receive the crown of life that God promised to those who love him." God will bless us with an abundant life even though we go through tough times, we just have to press forward. We will be victorious because He's promising us an eternal life. He is our hope. He is our strength. He is our redeemer.

Daniel encourages us to remain faithful to God regardless of what we face. The story begins with the king showing favor towards Daniel so the corrupt administrators brought before King Darius a decree which forbade anyone to worship anyone but the king for thirty days. They were jealous of Daniel and knew he worshipped God. So, when Daniel was caught praying, the king had no choice but to throw Daniel in the lion's den because the edict had been signed. When the king found Daniel alive and well the next morning, he re-issued another decree declaring the kingdom would worship the God who rescued Daniel.

So, during those uncertain times in our lives, we can trust God will always show up. He is able to turn an impossible situation where there is no hope into a beautiful story bringing Him honor. Even during the bleakest moments, we must remember *every cloud does have a silver lining* when our confidence is embedded in our Heavenly Father.

> *"Let us not become weary in doing good, for at the proper time we will reap a harvest if we do not give up."*
>
> Galatians 6:9

NO GOOD DEED GOES UNPUNISHED

No good deed goes unpunished is a sarcastic way of saying the more you do for someone the more they'll ask. This derives from several Scriptures which speak about doing good to others.

I love the concept of the Amish community. They exhibit the perfect example of what Paul is talking about in Galatians. If someone needs a new barn, they have a "barn raising", where everyone comes together and builds a barn. Regardless of the needs of a brother or sister in Christ, they jump in to do whatever they need to do.

We have become a selfish society, thinking only of ourselves. I've heard people say before they believe their religion is private and they don't feel comfortable sharing. As a believer in Christ, how are others going to know about Him if we don't share and sometimes the best way to share is simply to care. When we go out of our way to serve and help others, it takes the focus off ourselves, and we become a true servant for Christ.

Society may say, "*No good deed goes unpunished*", but we know our reward will be in heaven. Genuine faith produces good deeds because we become vessels of Christ when He comes into our heart. We become the instrument used to bring others to God. We will surely be blessed when we graciously help others because we are exemplifying our faith through our actions.

As believers, we cannot get tired of doing good because we know our chief purpose of existence is to glorify God in all we do and all we say. We may not ever see a harvest, but that's okay, we've just been called to plant the seed.

"He who conceals his sins does not prosper, but whoever confesses and renounces them finds mercy."

Proverbs 28:13

IF THE SHOE FITS, WEAR IT

If the shoe fits, wear it means if the criticism pertains to you, accept and learn from it. Different versions of this statement have been around for centuries, using "hats" or "cloaks". Some believe the "shoe" was interjected after the story of Cinderella which derived from the Italian folk tale *Cenerentola* in 1634.

During the ministry of Jesus, the blinders were pulled off the followers. He made them see for themselves their sinful way of life. When He confronted the Samaritan woman at the well, there was no judgment, only love and compassion. When Jesus made her see the reflection of her life, she fled from her sinful ways.

We are all fallible but when we acknowledge our mistakes and take responsibility, we learn from them and grow. It takes boldness to acknowledge our blunders and then repair the damage from our wrongdoing. Whether it's saying something about someone that hurts their feelings or doing something dishonest, we need to take ownership and make it right.

The older we get, the more set in our ways we become but I don't believe we're ever too old to improve on our personalities. None of us likes to be critiqued but when we are, we should accept it graciously and with humility. There's a growth which happens when we are able to receive constructive criticism and learn from it.

As believers we're called to lovingly call out each other and *if the shoe fits, we need to wear it* with grace. God puts others in our paths to help guide and teach us so we can continually improve. Galatians 6:1a says, "Brothers, if someone is caught in a sin, you who are spiritual should restore him gently." The key word here is "gently". The footnote to this verse is interesting because it says the Greek verb for restore is used to repair nets or setting bones.In other words, if we see someone in trouble, we're called to help repair their relationship with God, which sin has eroded.

"When words are many, sin is not absent, but he who holds his tongue is wise."

Proverbs 10:19

SHOOT FROM THE HIP

Shoot from the hip is an expressive way to say someone speaks without thinking or acts impulsively. This idiom originates from the wild west when cowboys would shoot their gun from their holster which would be less accurate.

Mama was one of the bluntest people I've ever known. She had absolutely no filter. If you didn't want an honest answer, you shouldn't have asked her a question. Unfortunately, I'm a lot like her in that regard but I know the Lord has convicted me to be more sensitive and really try to think before I speak. Our words are powerful and when we impulsively speak without considering how it will be received, the message can be hurtful. Our tongue has the power to build someone up or tear them down. As believers we're called to encourage one another and speak lovingly to those around us.

Our tongue is the mouthpiece of our heart. Whatever we harbor inside our heart will eventually overflow out of us because our tongue is the rudder of our souls and a reflection of our spirit. If we want others to be drawn closer to God, we have to guard what we say and the tone in which we say it. James 3:3-12 explains how destructive our words can be and how our small tongue has the ability to set the course of our entire body. As believers, we're called to tame our tongue to avoid corruption and evil.

James 1:26 gives a harsh truth about how powerful our words can be saying, "If anyone considers himself religious and yet does not keep a tight rein on his tongue, he deceives himself and his religion is worthless." We can't just callously *shoot from the hip* with gossip, slander, and ugly words spewing from our lips and call ourselves followers of Christ at the same time. We have to be set apart with a pure heart longing to please the Lord and be sensitive with our words so we never crush the spirit of others.

"His head and hair were white like wool, as white as snow, and his eyes were like blazing fire."

Revelation 1:14

PULL THE WOOL OVER YOUR EYES

Pulling the wool over someone's eyes means they're being deceived to be taken advantage of. This idiom comes from the days of wearing white powder wigs where street thugs would approach victims from behind and pull the wigs over their eyes before robbing them.

By nature, I'm very gullible. When someone says something to me, I believe it because I tell the truth and I expect them to do the same. I've been hurt when someone I trusted and really opened up to later betrayed me.

The Bible is full of warnings about deceitfulness because the world we live in is full of twisted truths and narratives to fit the agenda which the person is pushing. As believers we must test what we hear against the Word of God so we know the truth. The inerrant Word of God brings darkness to light and darkness can no longer exist in the light.

We have to remain prudent with a boldness coming only from God. Deception can creep into every crevice of our lives so as believers we must always stand for the truth. To know the truth, we must study the Scriptures and store them in our hearts.

As the world around us seems to become darker and darker, it's difficult to see the injustices and wickedness continue to prevail. But we can't lose heart and we must stay the course. As you read the later letters from Paul, he warns the churches about deception and false prophets becoming more prevalent as society deteriorated, much like what we see happening today.

As believers we have to remain constant in our faith regardless of what we see happening around us. We're able to stand firm because we have God's living Word embedded in our hearts, and as our faith grows, so does our discernment making it harder to *pull the wool over our eyes.*

"Awake, my soul! Awake, harp and lyre! I will awaken the dawn."

Psalm 57:8

UP AT THE CRACK OF DAWN

The idiom *up at the crack of dawn* means you are an early riser, starting your day before the sun even appears on the horizon.

I am an early riser. The older I get the less sleep I seem to require. Each morning is like the movie "Groundhog Day". I get up, let the dogs out, turn the coffee pot on, feed the dogs, then have my devotions.

Usually, mid-morning I head out for a walk with my girlfriend. The minute I put my shoes on, my dogs Piper and Cooper go crazy. They start pacing back and forth, then they swirl in circles because they anticipate a walk.

My dogs become gleeful at the mere possibility of a walk; you can physically see it. I want to be that excited about my daily walk with the Lord. Not necessarily swirling in circles but I want to have an uncontainable joy that overflows. A joy so complete others can see it.

I love how the Psalmist wrote this verse using exclamation marks. He's shouting, "AWAKE, MY SOUL! " He is singing praises before the day begins and using instruments to celebrate God's saving grace. We should all get up each day with a grateful heart. Spending time in the mornings with the Lord nourishes our souls and arms us for the day.

Psalm 23:1-3 reiterates how important quiet time is, "The Lord is my shepherd, I shall not be in want. He makes me lie down in green pastures, he leads me beside quiet waters, he restores my soul." David is metaphorically comparing us to sheep, with the Lord being the shepherd who tends His flock. A sheep only lies down when they're content and the calm water quenches their thirst. God's living Word does the same for us, it replenishes our souls and gives us a spirit of contentment. Reading Scripture prepares us to greet each day with excitement even if we are *up at the crack of dawn.*

> *"Then the angel showed me the river of the water of life, as clear as crystal, flowing from the throne of God and of the Lamb."*
>
> Revelation 22:1

CRYSTAL CLEAR

Crystal clear means something is absolutely transparent or is easily understood. This comes from the description of the water of life in the book of Revelation.

Have you ever tried to tell a story and somehow it got so misconstrued the point you were trying to make became confusing? I know I have! It's like I'm trying to get three ideas out of my mind at the same time, so they all get twisted en route from my brain to my lips. I have to stop, reboot, slow down and start again.

While Jesus was teaching, He never had an issue getting His point across. His messages were direct and straight to the point. He had the ability to keep the people hanging on every word when He spoke, touching their hearts and turning them into believers.

Throughout the ministry of Jesus, He never once contradicted himself. He spoke truth with love and compassion spreading the importance of becoming a Christ-follower. He continually reminded the people the source to true joy and contentment was to have faith in Him. He was sent to earth from our Heavenly Father to spare our souls with the promise of eternal life.

There is nothing we can do to earn our way into eternal life. It's a gift purchased by the blood of Christ; all we have to do is believe. And the moment we believe, we tap into the abundant living waters of Jesus which are everflowing and *crystal clear.*

"Our mouths were filled with laughter, our tongues with songs of joy."

Psalm 126:2a

HAPPY AS A LARK

Happy as a lark means to be filled with joy, gleeful, or lighthearted. Grandma said this to describe someone who was joyous and carefree. This comes from the fact a lark is known for it's beautiful melodious song which is pleasing to hear.

My parents did a great job of shielding me from the troubles that burdened them when I was a kid. I had a happy-go-lucky attitude without a care in the world. But as I got older, I would hear their concerns like making ends meet, the gas shortage, and other global issues so I began to worry about stuff I had no control over.

Worry robs us of our joy. It's very difficult to remain happy when we allow worries and concerns to weigh us down. The stronger I've grown in my faith, the more I have become dependent on the strength of God to console me. Life can get heavy, and it's easy to let anxious thoughts seep in.

I have two girlfriends I have known since high school. Although we live in different states and we are busy with our own families, when we get together, all we do is laugh. They accept me just as I am and we enjoy each other's company. The concerns of life sluff off our shoulders and our spirits are renewed. Just as my friends renew my spirit when I'm with them, God renews our spirits when we seek Him. He can be the constant source of our joy. Joy which is not fleeting and is not based on our circumstances because it is complete.

God wants us to have fellowship with others to build us up. When we surround ourselves with believers, our spirits are renewed and replenished. And even though life is troublesome at times, we can remain as *happy as a lark* when we give our worries to God.

"In all your ways acknowledge him, and he will make your paths straight."

Proverbs 3:6

CHALK IT UP TO

When someone says *chalk it up to* something, they're giving credit to someone else for their accomplishments or deflecting their responsibilities for their inadequacies. This originates from keeping a tab when buying things on credit by writing them down on slate with chalk.

All of our children have played on one sports team or another, ranging in all athletic abilities. We could always tell when they had really good coaches because our child would strive to meet the goals that had been set. They loved going to practice and improved during each game. A good coach would always acknowledge them coming off the field even when it wasn't our child's shining moment.

We sort of measure up to the expectations that have been set before us. Most of us like to please others and try our best at everything, but we like to be acknowledged for it too. We all like to be "stroked" with accolades and praises even as adults. It's easy to spot a great manager in a workplace because the morale and job performance of his employees reflect how well they are being supervised.

In 1 Chronicles 28, God has chosen David's son Solomon to succeed him on the throne. In verse 9, David reminds Solomon, "acknowledge the God of your Father, and serve him with wholehearted devotion... the Lord searches every heart and understands every motive behind the thoughts." David was reiterating the fact that Solomon would only be a successful king as long as he acknowledged God in his life.

We are influenced by so many things; our parents, workplace, relationships, media, environment, religion, and our own selfish desires just to name a few. God wants to be our "influencer". The only one we seek approval from because He is a jealous God. As we develop a relationship with Him, we are gently being molded into His likeness. Any good qualities in the person I am today, I have to *chalk it up to God's* grace and thankfully He's still working on me.

"I sought the Lord, and he answered me; he delivered me from all my fears."

Psalm 34:4

SCARED THE LIVING DAYLIGHTS OUT OF ME

When anyone uses the saying *scared the living daylights out of me,* they're extremely scared. The word daylights, is actually referring to the eyes of a person so to be this scared you have literally lost your sight.

I remember driving home from my parents' house one day and the winds picked up quickly as the skies grew dark and ominous. It was scary. The driving rain mixed with hail was pelting the car so hard I could barely see and all I could do was grab the wheel with white knuckles to stay on the road. As I prayed a calmness came over me and I was so thankful when I had driven past the storm cloud.

We all have to go through storms. Some are brief while others we have to endure for quite some time and we wonder when they will ever end. But when we get to the other side and reflect back, we see the grace of God carried us through.

We see this illustrated in Matthew 8:23-27 when the disciples were in a boat crossing the Sea of Galilee. Jesus slept as they sailed when all of a sudden, a furious storm approached. As the waves crashed over the boat, the fear grew in the disciples so they went to Jesus to wake him pleading to be saved. Jesus had to know they were in the midst of the storm so He could have calmed the seas before it got that bad. But He waited. He didn't act until the disciples came to Him and asked for help.

I think that's how it is in our lives sometimes. We think we can weather the storm on our own until it gets too bad and then we seek comfort from the Lord. Jesus wants us to call on Him before the storm even starts and not just ask for help when we're getting the living daylights scared out of us.

"He guides me in paths of righteousness for his name's sake."

Psalm 23:3

BLAZE YOUR OWN TRAIL

*Blaze your own trail i*s referring to someone creating their own path in life rather than following others. In the business world it refers to a more inventive method of doing things. This is an old saying originating from soldiers using their weapons to leave a trail of smoke and fire on trees along a path making it easier for others to follow.

    I love to hike and there are countless trails near us. Recently my girlfriend and I set out on a trail and the longer we walked the narrower the path became. Several trails branched off from the main path we were on so I can see how easy it would be to get lost in the woods if you didn't pay attention to the trail markings.

In life it's easy to take the wrong path especially when we try to do things our own way instead of seeking the direction from God. Psalm 119:105 says, "Your word is a lamp to my feet and a light for my path." Without light we have to grope about in the darkness because we cannot see.

The good news is no matter how far off the path we may stray, the Lord will always redirect our steps and shed light in the direction we're to take. Even when we are *blazing our own trail,* we're never alone. We can take comfort knowing God wants us to succeed in all we do. We can be trend-setters leading the way for others to follow especially when we allow God to guide us along the way.

"For the sinful nature desires what is contrary to the Spirit, and the Spirit what is contrary to the sinful nature. They are in conflict with each other, so that you do not do what you want."

Galatians 5:17

STICK IN THE MUD

A stick in the mud is a person who resists change and has a difficult time engaging in new activities. This analogy comes from feet or carriage wheels that would get bogged down in the mud and muck.

There are some things we like doing more than others but because of our love for those around us, we compromise. In some instances, I have gone along with doing activities I wasn't comfortable with, but I ended up actually enjoying, like snorkeling. I didn't want to be the only one in the group to stop the others from having fun.

The Pharisees had a difficult time accepting change and questioned why the disciples were not fasting. While Jesus was busy with His ministry, they couldn't understand why the disciples were not following the letter of the law. Jesus replies with a parable in Mark 2:22, "And no one pours new wine into old wineskins. If he does, the wine will burst the skins, and both the wine and the wineskins will be ruined. No, he pours new wine into new wineskins." Jesus is saying He's bringing a new way that cannot be confined by the old way.

Romans 15:13 says, "May the God of hope fill you with all joy and peace as you trust in him, so that you may overflow with hope by the power of the Holy Spirit." Simply put, when we have hope in the Lord it radiates from us. We have been called to be a beacon to illuminate and guide others.

When we put our hope and trust in the Lord, we don't have to be a *stick in the mud* and resist change. When we keep an open mind, we're allowing God to work through us on that next adventure. We have a loving Heavenly Father who will guide us every step of the way.

> "A wife of noble character who can find? She is worth far more than rubies."
>
> Proverbs 31:10

NOT WORTH A PLUG NICKEL

Not worth a plug nickel means something has no value; it is worthless. This comes from the practice of taking the valuable metal out of coins and making them worthless because they were tampered with.

I used to place my value in what my peers thought about me because I had no relationship with Jesus, so the world was my measuring stick. My confidence would fluctuate depending on how I was treated that day.

After I became a believer, I found a new confidence in myself. I no longer had to conform to the crowd to get validation. God chose me where I was, not where he wanted me to be. Paul reminds us in Philippians 1:6, "being confident in this, that he began a good work in you will carry it on to completion until the day of Christ Jesus." I love the fact it's actually written out that God has begun a good work in us and we will be "under construction" until the Lord returns.

If we're honest I think we all allow self-doubt to seep in from time to time and question our value. How can I be worthy of God's love? But then I remind myself Jesus came to save us all. In Luke 12:7, Jesus talks about how well God knows us and if he cares for the birds how much more he cares for us, "Indeed, the very hairs of your head are numbered. Don't be afraid; you are worth more than many sparrows."

We have been selected to join into the family of believers and were validated when we were redeemed. Now it is our responsibility to bring Him glory in all we do.

"Do not judge, or you too will be judged."

Matthew 7:1

YOU CAN'T JUDGE A BOOK BY ITS COVER

When anyone uses the idiom, *you can't judge a book by its cover,* they're saying you cannot form an opinion about anyone else by their outward appearance.

Once we had a preacher who told a beautiful story about a stranger who had come to visit a church. The man wore old, tattered clothes, had long shaggy hair, he was unshaven, and awkwardly sat alone in a pew. As the congregation filed into the pews, not one soul spoke to the lonely man. After the choir sang their final hymn, the man politely got up and approached the pulpit.

He was actually the pastor of the church who had disguised himself as a homeless man. The sermon that day was about judging others solely based on one's appearance. He made the congregation see how harshly he was treated as a homeless man. He was ignored, unwelcome, and never shown the love of Christ. The preacher gave a beautiful visual of how not to treat others. Every one of us is important to the Lord, and we all deserve to be treated with love and kindness.

Jesus gives us stern warnings regarding judging others. In the parable He asks in Luke 6:41, "Why do you look at the speck of sawdust in your brother's eye and pay no attention to the plank in your own eye?" Jesus is using the illustration to show the hypocrisy when we criticize others while having faults of our own. Not one of us is perfect, but with the grace of God we can ask for forgiveness when we mess up.

It's easy to love people who look and act like us but that's not what Jesus has called us to do. We *can't judge a book by its cover* because you never know what's on the inside until you crack it open.

"For if you forgive men when they sin against you, your heavenly Father will also forgive you."

Matthew 6:14

STUCK IN YOUR CRAW

If something is *stuck in your craw,* it means something is irritating or bothering you. This originates from the crop of a bird, the small storage pouch on the throat of the animal, which aids in their digestion. Birds will eat small stones to help digest their food but if they eat a large stone, it will get stuck.

Forgiveness is tricky. If we're honest, I don't think many of us ever feel like forgiving someone who has hurt or betrayed us. It's a conscious decision we decide to make because that's what Jesus tells us to do.

I broke a glass the other day and thought I cleaned it all up but apparently, I didn't because I ended up with a sliver in my foot. I thought I removed it but days later, my foot was still sore and now inflamed. Now I had no choice but to dig the glass out because it's infected and can actually go to my heart.

The same thing happens when we harbor resentment and hatred towards another person who has wronged us. They are living their life without giving us a second thought, meanwhile we're allowing all this anger to fester in our hearts. 1 Peter 4:8 reminds us of the power of love, "Above all, love each other deeply, because love covers over a multiple of sins." So, when we have anything *stuck in our craw,* we must choose to forgive and release ourselves from the bondage of resentment.

"rooted and built up in him, strengthened in the faith as you were taught, and overflowing with thankfulness."

Colossians 2:7

ROOT HOG OR DIE

Root hog or die is an old expression dating back to the colonial days. Farmers would let their pigs loose in the woods and they would literally have to forage for themselves to survive. Today it means you've got to work if you want to eat.

    I remember setting out on my own after college. It was both a scary and exciting endeavor to find an apartment, turn on the utilities, find a bank, etc., because all the responsibility was on me. I was totally on my own.

Hagar also set out on her own but not on her terms. She was an Egyptian maidservant belonging to Sarah. God had spoken to Abraham and told him he would produce an heir even in his old age. In Sarah's impatience, she took matters into her own hands and an heir was produced from Abraham, only the mother was Hagar.

Years later, God did fulfill His promise and gave Sarah a son, Isaac. As Hagar's son grew, so did the seed of jealousy which was planted in Sarah's heart. Hagar was rejected, mistreated, and banished into the desert where she had to fend for herself to survive. The life she once knew no longer existed, but the Lord heard Ishmael's cries and saved them both.

Most of us have been in our own desert at some point. Whether it is health issues, losing a loved one, or some other traumatic situation we're navigating through, God hears us.

We are girded with His strength which enables us to endure anything when we're rooted in His Word. He is constant and ever present when we call on Him. When we find ourselves in the "deserts" of life, God will never leave us to *root hog or die*. He is our oasis giving us rest, comfort, and a reprieve when we seek Him as our refuge.

> *"He who gathers crops in summer is a wise son, but he who sleeps during harvest is a disgraceful son."*
>
> Proverbs 10:5

MAKE HAY WHILE THE SUN SHINES

Making hay while the sun shines is an old proverbial saying deriving from Proverbs 10:5 which means to seize the opportunity while it lasts so you can make the most of it.

I know first-hand how important it is to get the hay up out of the field as quickly as possible. Daddy would do his best to watch the weather so he could get it in the barn before it rained. I love it when we're given a window of opportunity that is unexpected. There is something we need or want to do and then out of nowhere the opportunity presents itself. Some call it a coincidence, I call it God's providence. I believe God gives us these windows to reveal His goodness to others.

There's a Latin phrase "Carpe Diem", which means "Seize the day". In other words, make the best out of what you have been given. I believe God is constantly giving us chances throughout our ordinary day to do something extraordinary. He wants us to be the light in this dark world. We are called to stand out.

Isn't that what we're supposed to do? Squeeze all the goodness we can out of each day, then get up and do it all over again. When we live a life which is abundant with God's love, it overflows to others around us, we can't help it.

I saw this picture I just loved. It had a cup half full for the optimist, half empty for the pessimist, and the cup overflowing in reference to Psalm 23:5 saying, "my cup runneth over." (KJV). It's all about our perspective on how we view each day. I want to be the overflowing cup so I can splash God's goodness and grace on those I come in contact with. So, in the course of our day, we all need to *make hay while the sun shines* and seize every opportunity God gives us to reveal His love to others.

> "For I am the Lord, your God, who takes hold of your right hand and says to you, Do not fear; I will help you."
>
> Isaiah 41:13

IN OVER YOUR HEAD

In over your head means you're attempting to do a task beyond your capabilities. This is an analogy of someone who can't swim and is in water way too deep.

I am not a strong swimmer, so I am not comfortable swimming in deep water. When I was a kid, I went to church camp and on day one, we had to take a swimming test. The lake was divided by a "T" shaped pier separating the shallow side from the deeper side. I barley passed the skills test to swim in the deep side so I never swam over there.

Mama couldn't swim at all and she always made the joke she wasn't allowed in the water until she learned how to swim. We would never learn anything new if we always allowed fear to hold us back.

When Moses was approached by God to deliver the Israelites, he was overwhelmed to say the least. He made up all kinds of excuses and even asked God to send someone else because he was not an eloquent speaker. He may have been inadequate but with God he was more than capable.

God had faith in Moses to take on this daunting task, but Moses had to engage and obey. He was reassured God would be with him. Joshua 1:5 promises, "No one will be able to stand up against you all the days of your life. As I was with Moses, so I will be with you; I will never leave you nor forsake you." Just as God was with them, He is with us today.

When I think I have taken on a task that is *over my head,* I need to remember to trust God because His strength is revealed when I am weak. Instead of relying on the sandy bottom of the lake for security, I now rely on Christ. He is the source of my strength, my hope, and the rock I stand on.

"Do not lie to each other, since you have taken off your old self with its practices"

Colossians 3:9

GIVE YOU A PIECE OF MY MIND

When anyone says, "I'm *going to give you a piece of my mind"*, they are going to honestly say what they're thinking even though it may hurt one's feelings.

No one likes the conversation which starts out with, "We need to talk". You know something heavy is about to be said so you brace yourself for what's coming. I've had to be the bearer of bad news and it's not fun. I'm not confrontational and I like to avoid difficult conversations all together but, when there is a difference of opinion sometimes the air needs to be cleared to move forward. This can cause tension in the room and sometimes leads to resentment.

The first example of a confrontation in the Bible is right after Adam and Eve were caught red-handed in their sin. God goes directly to the point and asks in Genesis 3:11, "Who told you that you were naked? Have you eaten from the tree that I commanded you not to eat from?" God, being all knowing, starts the conversation by asking where they were, but he already knew. He was calling them out for their disobedience because the fellowship they once had with God was severed. They were now full of shame because they were embarrassed for what they had done.

They made a choice and we still have the same option today. We can have a relationship with God and obey His commandments or we can go our separate way. Even though we choose to follow Christ, sometimes we're put in awkward situations without knowing what to say but the Lord will give us the words when we ask.

As believers, we're set apart from the world. The truth is our sword that cuts through all lies and deception because we have been made new. Just as the caterpillar transforms into the butterfly, the moment we accept Jesus as our savior, we begin to shed the old self and put on the new.

> *"Where there are no oxen, the manger is empty, but from the strength of an ox comes an abundant harvest."*
>
> Proverbs 14:4

STRONG AS AN OX

The idiom *strong as an ox* obviously comes straight from Scripture and it means someone is extremely strong. Oxen are male castrated cattle known for their strength and docile demeanor. They were the tractor of the past used to farm the land.

Strength is not always physical; it can also be exhibited through an emotional trial. We have all been through something which is difficult, some more so than others. Regardless of the circumstance, what is the source of our strength when we're in the midst of these storms? By nature, everyone reacts differently, that's how God created us. Some run straight to God on a bent knee while others flee and become angry with God for allowing them to be put in the situation in the first place.

The entire book of Ephesians is written to encourage and strengthen the people, giving them a blueprint of how to live their lives. Paul is reminding the early church to stay focused on Christ so the love and grace of God will be revealed through their actions.

We have to remember when we feel like we can't go on any longer and the burden has become too great, we can become *as strong as an ox* when we seek the Lord. Paul totally understood the strength of God because he suffered an unimaginable amount of pain throughout his ministry.

Unlike Paul, who said he was delighted in his hardships, I wouldn't be honest if I said, "I can't wait for the next trial to come my way." But I can be comforted to know when it does come, I'll be as *strong as an ox* when my strength comes from the Lord. When we are equipped with the Holy Spirit, we're growing in His grace and hopefully reflecting the love of God.

" As for God, his way is perfect; the word of the Lord is flawless. "

Psalm 18:30a

YOU'RE THE BEE'S KNEES

You're the bee's knees means someone or something is excellent, perfect, or outstanding. The analogy comes from the actual knee of a bee which is microscopic, but made with complete detail and accuracy. The honey bee actually has pollen baskets called corbicula on the back of their legs to transport pollen.

Every intricate feature of these insects are wonderfully made specific to their needs, made perfect by God. If he cares so much about the minute details of an insect, how much more must he care for us.

Psalm 139:15 reminds us of how awesome our Creator is, "My frame was not hidden from you when I was made in the secret place. When I was woven together in the depths of the earth,". We are God's handiwork, hand-crafted by the One who made heaven and earth. God knew us while we were still in the womb, before we ever reached our mothers' arms. We were created in His image, so we have nothing but potential!

Because of the sin nature of man, we are flawed and far from perfection. But when Jesus was speaking to the crowds, He set the standard of what we should try to achieve, which is to mimic Christ. Although we will never achieve perfection while on this earth, Jesus is asking us to strive to reach it anyway.

In the eyes of God, we are all *the bee's knees*. We are uniquely created to bring Him glory and show those around us what it means to have a relationship with Jesus. He has given us each a talent we can use to bring Him glory. When we show unconditional love to others, especially the undeserving, we are the living testament the Holy Spirit is dwelling within us.

"restraining her is like restraining the wind or grasping oil with the hand."

Proverbs 27:16

GRASPING AT STRAWS

The idiom *grasping at straws* describes a desperate attempt to save yourself from trouble or not having a tangible method to succeed. This comes from an old proverb about a drowning person who will try to grab anything to save himself, even the reeds growing along the shoreline.

I grew up in the country and my summers were spent at Sinclair's Pond. This was where all the families in our community gathered to cool off on those hot days. I remember once I jumped off the end of the dock and a girl jumped on top of me while I was still under water. I struggled to get to the surface but the harder I tried the more entangled I became with her. These were dark waters so no one could see my desperate attempt to get air. I obviously made it out of the water but it was a very terrifying experience.

For most of us there have been times when we have felt desperate. The feeling we were sinking and we couldn't seem to find a way out. In these times we can feel terrified, isolated, and hopeless, especially when others don't know we are struggling.

David knew all too well what it was like to be in distress. Psalm 69:1-2 says, "Save me, O God, for the waters have come up to my neck. I sink in the miry depths, where there is no foothold." The image reminds me of what it must feel like to be in quicksand. He can't grasp onto anything to save himself, so he cries to the Lord in desperation. He knows only God's mercy can save him. He's hopeless because his circumstances have overwhelmed him.

I can remember feeling like David and retrospectively seeing God's grace again and again in my life, even before I was a believer. His loving arms protected me when I wasn't even aware of it and used those circumstances in my life to nudge me closer and closer to Him.

"From the fruit of his mouth a man's stomach is filled;"

Proverbs 18:20

PUT YOUR MONEY WHERE YOUR MOUTH IS

When anyone is told to *put their money where their mouth is,* they are being told to back up their words by taking action. This is believed to have originated from individuals with power, being challenged by others to back their words by spending their own cash.

I think we have to guard ourselves about becoming complacent and lazy. James reminds the believers that having faith without action is worthless. James 1:23 says, "Anyone who listens to the word but does not do what it says is like a man who looks at his face in a mirror and, after looking at himself, goes away and immediately forgets what he looks like." If no one knows you have a personal relationship with Jesus, then you aren't leading others to follow Him.

James is reiterating the fact we can't call ourselves followers of Christ if others around us have no idea we're Christians. We are called to be a beacon of light in this dark world and spiritual purity is reflected from us when we are illuminated by the Holy Spirit. We can say we're believers all day long but unless we hear God's Word and act on it, we're just someone who attends church.

When we become a believer, we become a part of the body of Christ. We are working in unison with Christ and just like a body part, it cannot function if it becomes unattached. We're able to reach those in need around us and serve others with a loving heart because of the Holy Spirit prompting us.

Genuine faith is demonstrated through our righteous actions. We are called to *put our money where our mouth is* and become the hands and feet of Christ. We have to let others see by our words and our deeds we belong to Christ and we're willing to serve Him when we're called into action.

> *"You hem me in—behind and before; you have laid your hand upon me."*
>
> Psalm 139:5

HEM AND HAW

Hem and haw can mean you have a difficult time making up your mind, you are indecisive, or it's said when someone pauses and hesitates when they speak. Both words hem and haw have similar meanings; to hesitate or stammer, so by putting the two words together it evolved into the idiom used today.

I remember when I was in the eighth grade, the worst day of the month was when we had to give our oral book reports. I felt physically ill because I was painfully shy and standing in the front of my class was terrifying. I had always read the book but getting my point across was not an easy task. It was like there was a disconnect between my brain and my mouth. Once I was so nervous, I rocked the podium back and forth so much it crashed to the floor.

I will never be an eloquent speaker, but thankfully I did outgrow my awkward shyness. I was asked to speak once in front of a group of ladies and all I could think about was how I had the entire class cracking up laughing at me so long ago. After much deliberation, I agreed to do it. I prepared what I was to say, and prayed God would give me the confidence I needed.

I was a nervous wreck as I approached the podium but as I began to speak, the words flowed from my lips without any hesitation. You see, my friend had given me a verse and told me to stand on His promise. My fear vanished and an unbelievable calmness came over me.

I learned a valuable lesson that day. When I am at my weakest, God's strength is revealed. When I think I can't do something, that's when God shows up and carries me through it.

Philippians 4:13 promises, "I can do everything through him who gives me strength." He is the supernatural strength equipping us to do what we think is impossible.

> *"If anyone considers himself religious and yet does not keep a tight rein on his tongue, he deceives himself and his religion is worthless."*
>
> James 1:26

LOOSE LIPS SINK SHIPS

Loose lips sink ships comes from a WWII ad campaign reminding Americans to beware of an unbridled tongue so information didn't get back to the enemy. Today it's used when someone has a blabbermouth.

The heart and the tongue are definitely connected, because what fills our hearts flows from our lips. The tongue is such a small part of our body, but it has the power to build someone up or break them down in an instant.

I remember when I was in third grade, and I was making jokes about my friend wearing glasses. I felt awful because I really hurt her feelings and made her cry, then I cried. Careless words hurt and leave scars taking longer to heal than physical wounds sometimes.

James compares the tongue to the rudder of a ship. Regardless of how large the ship may be, it can be steered in high seas and strong winds using the very small device attached to any vessel. Likewise, the tongue sets the course for the whole body because we're known by our words, and we're called to guard against evil.

Refraining from foolish talk makes you wiser and keeps you from saying something you shouldn't. I love the verse Proverbs 17:28, "Even a fool is thought wise if he keeps silent, and discerning if he holds his tongue." There's a popular phrase which comes from this Scripture saying, "It's better to be thought a fool than to open your mouth and prove them right."

Our Sunday school teacher gave an illustration of the tube of toothpaste. Once the paste is squeezed out of the tube, you can't just put it back in. The same goes with our words. Once we've said something insensitive, it's hard to repair the damage. We need to be kind and thoughtful when we speak and remember *loose lips do sink ships* and wreck relationships.

"He will be like rain falling on a mown field, like showers watering the earth."

Psalm 72:6

WHEN IT RAINS IT POURS

The idiom *when it rains it pours* alludes to when a sequence of good **or bad** events happens in our life. This is more commonly used when **a string** of unfortunate things happens. This was actually a successful **ad campaign** for Morton Salt Company in the early 1900's.

Sometimes one event that happens in our life can have a ripple effect causing multiple other events to follow. That was the case for our daughter several years ago. Within a very short span of time, she found out she was getting divorced, losing her home, and her job. Life as she knew it no longer existed, so she had to make adjustments quickly.

Nowhere in the Scriptures does it promise life is going to be all lollipops and rainbows. But because God sent His only Son to pardon our sins, we have the promise of hope. Hope for a brighter future because we know that no matter what obstacles we face, we're never alone.

When we keep in mind our blessings, we quickly realize even when things seem like they can't get any worse, they actually could if it wasn't for God's grace. When we turn our hearts to the Lord, it changes the trajectory of our attitudes and gives us a grateful spirit.

Often we don't see our blessings until we have weathered the storm. We take so much for granted, not appreciating it until we lose it. But the Lord is faithful to those who believe and will restore us. We usually get drenched when we get caught in a storm but the Lord is like an umbrella keeping us dry. God promises a blessed life to His people.

So, when the storm clouds roll in on the horizon, we can stand firm on the Rock, knowing even when it's pouring rain, we can have the peace that passes all understanding when we seek Him for shelter.

"This is the day that the Lord has made; let us rejoice and be glad in it."

Psalm 118:24

BRIGHT-EYED AND BUSHY-TAILED

Early publications indicate *bright-eyed and bushy-tailed* was used to describe a squirrel but today it refers to someone who is eager, cheerful, and full of energy. I remember hearing this as a kid when I jumped out of bed eager to start the day.

You're either a morning person or not. I habitually get up very early, but I've got a friend who drags herself out of bed and stumbles into the kitchen to get that first cup of coffee.

There are many adjectives which can be used to describe this idiom: enthusiastic, energetic, earnest, perky, happy, and zealous just to name a few. That's the kind of Christian God wants us to be. He wants us to have a zest for this life, eager to share His Word and serve others.

As I'm digging through the Scriptures looking up enthusiasm, I find the word zeal is used. To be zealous about anything is to do it with passion, diligence, devotion, and eagerness. Romans 12:11 says, "Never be lacking in zeal, but keep your spiritual fervor, serving the Lord." Fervor means to have an intense and passionate feeling. So not only should we be zealous to serve the Lord but always remember to show Him reverence.

We're not always going to be *bright-eyed and bushy-tailed* in all we do, but we can be eager to bring Him glory. When we're working to please God, He gives us the desire to be "all-in", without any reservation or hesitation regardless of what we're doing.

> *"Jesus answered, I am the way and the truth and the life. No one comes to the Father except through me."*
>
> John 14:6

CUT TO THE CHASE

The idiom *cut to the chase* means to get to the point and skip the unimportant part. This is believed to have originated from the movie industry. Most movies had an epic chase scene and when the film was edited, they would say, "Cut to the chase".

Have you ever been watching a movie and it's just so predictable you have a hard time staying interested? I find my mind starts drifting because I have lost interest.

While Jesus was teaching, He never had the problem of being boring. He was charismatic and always attracted a crowd. Jesus knew there was only a short time to get the message which needed to be delivered out and He often used parables to teach the people real life scenarios rather than just tell them what to do. He made it simple so everyone could understand and then they could implement biblical principles into their own lives.

Jewish law was complex and regimented but Jesus freed us all from the doctrines which had bound the faithful for years. His mission was to let everyone know that anyone who believes in Him shall have eternal life. We can never be good enough to earn our way into heaven ... it is only by God's grace we receive the free gift of salvation; we just have to believe.

Jesus came to earth and *cut to the chase* on how we can get to heaven. He broke the barriers. He never saw race and only saw the human heart needing help. He came to save, serve, and love mankind in order to bridge the gap between God and man.

The second chapter of Philippians is a beautiful blueprint of how we should live our lives. As we grow in our faith, so does our intimate relationship with Christ because we are relying on His strength and not our own. Philippians 2:5 sums it up, "Your attitude should be the same as that of Jesus Christ." When we constantly keep a Christ-like attitude we're witnessing to everyone we meet.

> *"For the Son of Man came to seek and to save what was lost."*
>
> Luke 19:10

A LOST CAUSE

When anyone says *it's a lost cause*, they're basically surrendering because the possibility of success is improbable. They have lost all hope of completing the task or having a positive outcome to a situation. Another way to say the same thing is *cut your losses*, meaning to stop.

I'm so thankful God has never given up and tossed me aside. I know I've disappointed Him and not measured up at times but He still loves me. His love is never changing and is always in pursuit of His children.

Jesus tells a beautiful parable revealing just how much God loves each and every one of us no matter where we are. Luke 15:4 says, "Suppose one of you has a hundred sheep and loses one of them. Does he not leave the ninety-nine in the open country and go after the lost sheep until he finds it?" The shepherd is so excited about finding his lost sheep he calls his friends and neighbors to celebrate.

I just love that! God seeks us when we've gone astray and carries us back to the fold draped across His shoulders like a shepherd carries his sheep. He doesn't leave us out there with the wolves who are waiting to devour us. Even when we lose our way and fall into sin, our Father is there to save us from imminent danger. This story demonstrates how much love God has for us, a love so deep, it's hard to even comprehend.

Once we're a child of God, we become a part of His flock. Although we are believers, sometimes we lose our way and stray. We focus on other things, reprioritize our relationship with God and lose fellowship with Jesus. When we keep God at the center of our lives, we stay on track and are equipped to weather the storms confronting us along the way. We're never a *lost cause* in the eyes of God, He never gives up on us.

> *"For we are God's workmanship, created in Christ Jesus to do good works, which God prepared in advance for us to do."*
>
> Ephesians 2:10

A PIECE OF WORK

To be called *a piece of work,* you are a complex, interesting, and unique individual. Shakespeare actually used the term in Hamlet referring to man.

My sister-in-law has become a master quilter. Not only does she create these beautiful pieces of art, but she is also an instructor to others. She masterfully crafts small pieces of fabric into a finished masterpiece, with no two the same.

We too are wonderfully made by a God who loves us beyond measure. We are one of a kind, an original which cannot be replicated. Psalm 139:13 says, "For you created my inmost being; you knit me together in my mother's womb." I love the image of God knitting me together cell by cell. The footnote in my Bible refers to the inmost being as a Hebrew idiom meaning "kidneys" as in the innermost center of moral sensitivity and emotions. God is our moral compass already woven into us as we're being formed in the womb. We are all made in His likeness, however because we've been given free will, we ultimately have the choice as to whom we will serve. We either love the Lord with our whole heart or we conform to the world.

As believers, we are to imitate God and we do this by living a harmonious life filled with love. God longs for us to continually be a work in progress, pushing to become more and more like Him.

We have all been given a special talent and we're to use these talents to glorify God. So even though we are flawed and far from perfection, the Lord can use us when we have a willing spirit.

We are all a unique *piece of work* created by the Creator of the universe. He has started a work in us which will continually grow more and more into His likeness.

"Your righteousness is like the mighty mountains,"

Psalm 36:6a

MAKE A MOUNTAIN OUT OF A MOLEHILL

To m*ake a mountain out of a molehill* is to turn a small issue into a big problem needlessly. This is an old proverbial saying which has been around for centuries.

Little kids are the worst at turning every little thing into a traumatic event. Their nature is to get attention from us so for dramatic effect, small boo boos and bumps draw big tears. That is if we allow it. When my children would get hurt, I'd calmly say, "Are you bleeding?" Nine times out of ten no blood was involved so it was nothing a soft kiss couldn't cure.

As adults we can be like that too. I knew someone who always wanted the focus of attention to be on her so drama seemed to follow her wherever she went. I remember one time she even pretended to faint for dramatic effect.

When Jesus met with the crowds, exaggerations were used for dramatic effect to get His point across. Matthew 23:24 says, "You strain out a gnat but swallow a camel." Simply put it means you neglect the important issues while paying attention to the most minute ones. It's all about keeping things in perspective and not getting tunnel vision.

Every day we all face different issues, some larger and more problematic than others. But when we keep them in perspective and don't *make a mountain out of a molehill,* we won't become frustrated and overwhelmed by the trivial things we have to deal with. When God is the priority in our lives, our views regarding the things on this earth change and our focus becomes more about pleasing Him.

"We are hard pressed on every side, but not crushed; perplexed, but not in despair;"

2 Corinthians 4:8

HARD-PRESSED

Hard-pressed means to struggle to accomplish whatever you have set out to do. There just doesn't seem to be enough time to get the job done. I just love it when I find one of these idioms I've grown up hearing originates from the Bible. This is from Paul speaking to Corinth about being able to withstand pressure without being crushed.

Mama loved to can vegetables and make jellies, pickles and relish. It's great she enjoyed canning, but making jelly is something I never enjoyed. She would cook the fruit and then it had to be pressed through this cone-shaped colander to eliminate all the seeds. The end product was excellent, but the process was very time consuming.

Whether it's the feeling of being inadequate to accomplish a task or whether it's just having enough time in the day to squeeze in one more thing, we all experience pressure.

One of the most sought out jewels in the world is the diamond. It's classified as a rare stone known for its brilliance and durability and has become a symbol of love. It is formed from years and years of intense pressure to carbon causing crystals to grow forming these luxurious stones and the end result is one of the hardest most beautiful gems.

In 2 Corinthians 4:8, Paul is talking about "being hard pressed on every side, but not crushed; perplexed, but not in despair; persecuted, but not abandoned; struck down, but not destroyed." We, like a diamond, become refined when we endure great pressure. As believers we have the Holy Spirit residing in us, so we can bear the trials we face without ever losing hope. Hope for a brighter future and hope for an eternal life.

Regardless of how hard-pressed we are, we can know with certainty we'll not be crushed. When we seek guidance and assistance from God to equip us, we're able to persevere. Perseverance builds our character as we're growing in our relationship with Christ.

"Mockers stir up a city, but wise men turn away anger."

Proverbs 29:8

A FISH OUT OF WATER

A fish out of water refers to a situation where someone is not comfortable with their surroundings or feels awkward when asked to do a certain activity. This analogy comes from the fact a fish will quickly die when not in water.

Most of us want to "fit in" and to be included, I know I do. I went through the awkward middle school years like so many others. I had friends, but I wouldn't be classified as popular by any stretch of the imagination.

I can still remember the embarrassment of having to change for gym class. We were required to "dress out" in this hideous polyester uniform. Most girls were developed or well on their way and I looked like "Flat Stanley". Once changed, I had to subject myself to further humiliation when we played team sports. I admit I had the athletic ability of a post, and I basically looked like one too but I did try my best. It was usually me and one other non-athletic kid who were the last ones picked. I can still hear them say, "Nope, we had her last time".

It's so ironic that as a kid, all I ever wanted was to be chosen, to belong to a group and to be included. Now as a believer, Jesus has called us to be set apart, to stand out and not follow the crowd. Romans 12:2a says, "Do not conform any longer to the pattern of this world, but be transformed by the renewing of your mind." This simply means the Lord changes the way we think.

When we feel like *a fish out of water* in a crowd where we don't fit in, it's okay. We are chosen. We have been selected by the Creator of heaven and earth to be an active member of His team.

"But when he asks, he must believe and not doubt, because he who doubts is like a wave of the sea, blown and tossed by the wind."

James 1:6

WISHY WASHY

When a person lacks strength making up their mind or changes their opinions often, they may be called *wishy washy*. This is an old idiom meaning to be watered down.

I don't have a problem giving my opinion, in fact I get in trouble sometimes because I'm too honest. Biblical truths are ingrained in me and woven into who I am, they are the foundation on which I base all of my opinions. However true this statement may be, I need to be mindful I don't come across judgmental.

In Matthew 26:34, Jesus tells Peter he will deny him, "I tell you the truth, Jesus answered, this very night, before the rooster crows, you will disown me three times." Even Peter, one of Jesus's very own disciples, failed to stand up for Christ. He allowed fear to stifle the truth.

In the world we live in today, we see countless truths getting trampled upon. We look around and see how others have twisted the truth to fit their narrative and they say one thing yet do another. Standing on biblical principles takes boldness and courage which can only come from the Holy Spirit.

As believers, we're called to stand firm in our faith but we are never alone. We have to muster up the courage to face our fears and continue to move in the direction God is leading us. The world may criticize us but we can be encouraged through the Word of God.

Standing firm on biblical truths keeps us from being *wishy washy* and reading God's Word equips us to stand against the world. Ephesians 4:14 says, "Then we will no longer be infants, tossed back and forth by the waves, and blown here and there by every wind of teaching and by the cunning and craftiness of men in their deceitful scheming."

"She is more precious than rubies; nothing you desire can compare with her."

Proverbs 3:15

A DIAMOND IN THE ROUGH

If a person is referred to as *a diamond in the rough*, it means they have good character traits but lack etiquette, style, or manners. This is said because a diamond is just another unearthed rock until it is polished and cut, and it's often mistaken for quartz.

Several years ago, we went camping at Fairy Stone State Park. Legend has it when Christ was crucified, fairies began to cry and as their tears hit the earth, they crystallized and formed crosses. My friend and I decided we had to go on the hunt for some of these crosses. We drove to this special spot where the stones are unearthed after rainstorms and there, we began our quest to dig for these special rocks. At first all I could see were mud encrusted pebbles all looking the same. But as I started to see past the misshaped rock, I began to notice the image of the cross within. Once I found one and I realized what I was looking for, I began to find more and more.

It reminded me of how God saw me before I became a believer. I was just stuck in the muck of this world without a purpose, but God saw past my unworthy self and chose me anyway. He didn't wait until I was polished but rather looked within to reach me right where I was.

I think of Saul, who actually persecuted Christians. In an instant, he was converted right where he was on the road to Damascus and turned into one of Jesus's most beloved followers. Acts 9:15 says, "Go! This man is my chosen instrument to carry my name before the Gentiles and their kings and before the people of Israel." Jesus appeared to Saul after His resurrection making him a mouthpiece for the "great commission" and Paul became one of the great authors of the New Testament.

By the grace of God, I have been redeemed. I didn't deserve it, and I certainly didn't earn it. And even though we're still a work in progress or *a diamond in the rough,* on the day we reach glory we'll be like a perfectly cut diamond.

"When times are good, be happy; but when times are bad, consider: God has made the one as well as the other."

                                              Ecclesiastes 7:14

A RIPPLE EFFECT

A ripple effect means one event in your life caused a sequence of events to follow due to the repercussions of the first. This is a metaphor of throwing a rock into water.

More often than not, one bad decision can have a devastating effect in our life causing catastrophic consequences, leaving us wondering, "When will this end?" These events in our lives can leave us depleted and hopeless. We have to keep our faith, and when we get through the event, we can reflect and hopefully learn from our mistakes.

Life is complicated sometimes, and let's face it, it's just not fair. Bad things happen to good people but there is nothing in the Bible ever promising life will be fair. But it does however promise again and again God will never leave, abandon, or forsake us. Our attitude during these unsettling times in our lives can be a pivotal moment in the life of others around us when they see how we handle ourselves.

In James 1:2, he talks about how we're to handle the hardships we will endure and it strikes me when James says when we face "many kinds" of trials. He's basically trying to prepare us that life is going to have some potholes along the way, so we need to prepare for them by seeking godly wisdom.

It's easy to give praise and thanks to God when good things keep happening to us, but we need to look for the lesson we're supposed to be learning when things are not going well. When we continually give God praise in the midst of a trial, we're reflecting God's glory to those around us. We're the living Bible to the unbelievers around us.

Nothing is too big for God even when we can't seem to stop *the ripple effect* we've started. One problem seems to lead to another hurdle but we can rest when we put our hope in the Lord.

"Therefore come out from them and be separate, says the Lord. Touch no unclean thing, and I will receive you."

2 Corinthians 6:17

COMING OUT OF THE WOODWORK

When someone uses the phrase *coming out of the woodwork*, it's usually referring to people suddenly appearing when previously they were out of sight. For instance, everyone shows up after all the food has been prepared. This originally came from pests hiding in baseboards and woodwork.

I enjoy refinishing old furniture so I'm not afraid of a challenge. Upon one of my outings, I found this antique child's wardrobe for only twenty-five dollars. It was in horrible shape, but it had good bones so I knew it had potential and who doesn't love a deal?

When I got my treasure home, I put it in our back storage room and started applying the refinishing chemicals. Within minutes of application, hundreds of insects began to swarm out of this furniture. What had I done? I had just infested our house with all these bugs! I slammed the door shut and ran inside all upset and explained to my husband what was going on. I'm all frazzled and he just calmly says, "We'll just go get a bug bomb." Problem solved!

I was a lot like that old wardrobe before Christ came into my life. I was infested with negative thoughts and selfish ways because I was not making God a priority in my life. From the outside appearance I was happy, but on the inside, I was a mess.

I will never forget the inner peace I received the day I gave my life to Jesus, I received a transformation I really can't articulate into words. A sense of contentment and purpose filled my spirit. Isaiah 35:10 says, "and the ransomed of the Lord will return. They will enter Zion with singing; everlasting joy will crown their heads. Gladness and joy will overtake them, and sorrow and sighing will flee away."

> *"A hot-tempered person stirs up dissension, but a patient man calms a quarrel."*
>
> Proverbs 15:18

MADDER THAN A WET HEN

Madder than a wet hen means someone is angry or hard to get along with. This saying comes from the rumor farmers would dunk their chickens in water to break them from sitting on an empty nest. Even after the eggs were gathered, a hen would continue to sit on the nest and not lay any more eggs. Obviously, dunking her made her mad, but it would break the cycle and she'd start laying eggs again.

We have probably all been around someone who just seemed like they wanted to pick a fight. Regardless of what the topic of conversation is, they are confrontational and argumentative. As I've gotten older, I have chosen to distance myself from personalities who don't have a calming spirit.

We all get angry and upset at times. Even Jesus got angry when He entered the temple and drove out all who were buying and selling there. He displayed His anger by overturning the tables set up to sell doves for sacrifices. He was so upset because God was not being honored and the temple was disrespected.

When we receive Jesus as our Savior, the Holy Spirit equips us with the fruit of the spirit. Galatians 5:22 promises, "But the fruit of the Spirit is love, joy, peace, patience, kindness, goodness, faithfulness,… ." Notice it is singular "fruit" not "fruits". When we claim the fruit of the Spirit, we get all the goodness, not just one section. We now have the power of the Holy Spirit at our fingertips when we seek His guidance.

The Holy Spirit living inside us produces Christian virtues in our lives so we can become a living testimony for others to see. So, the more our faith grows, the more we're going to reflect the characteristics of Christ and not go around *madder than a wet hen*.

"And do not forget to do good and to share with others, for with such sacrifices God is pleased."

Hebrews 13:16

ACTIONS SPEAK LOUDER THAN WORDS

When we say *actions speak louder than words* to someone, we are reminding them how they act reveals their true character, regardless of what they may say.

We all have different ways of expressing our love to another. I went to a women's conference once and one of the guest speakers talked about "filling our tanks". Her entire segment was about the many different gestures we can do for each other to physically show our love. It may be making a perfect cup of coffee every morning or bringing in the paper. For her it was the fact her husband literally kept her gas tank full because she hated to pump gas.

The point she was making was to remind us to put others before ourselves. We can say "I love you" all day long but the words fall flat when our actions don't back it up.

Abraham was one of the most righteous men in the Old Testament. He was actually referred to as, "God's friend". But Abraham was put to the ultimate test when God asked him to sacrifice his long-awaited son Isaac. The love and adoration he had for his son was undeniable but his love for God was greater and he validated his love when he was willing to take his son's life. God saw how faithful Abraham was with his willing spirit and provided a ram caught in the thorns to be sacrificed instead of his beloved son Isaac.

James gives us stern warnings about how our faith and deeds work hand in hand. James 2:17 says, "In the same way, faith by itself, if it is not accompanied by action, is dead." As believers, faith and deeds are codependent and can't function alone successfully. When I physically love others, *my actions are speaking louder than words.*

> *"Like a bad tooth or a lame foot is reliance on the unfaithful in times of trouble."*
>
> Proverbs 25:19

LONG IN THE TOOTH

The phrase *long in the tooth* means something or someone has some age on it. This is believed to have originated from the fact you can estimate how old a horse is by the length of his teeth, the longer the teeth, the older the horse.

Both of my parents had horrible teeth, and eventually they ended up wearing dentures. One morning Mama was getting ready to go to work and when she placed her dentures in her mouth they wouldn't fit. She worked and worked trying to get them to fit but somehow her gums must have changed overnight because they DID NOT FIT. She was in a panic because there was no way she could go into work toothless. She woke Daddy up explaining the situation and he busted out laughing; she was trying to fit his dentures into her mouth!

If we live long enough, we all grow old. As the gray hairs start to sprout and the wrinkles start to show, we can physically see ourselves progressing in the aging process. Some of us age with grace, embracing the transformation while others resist it fighting tooth and nail. That's why the market is flooded with wrinkle creams, hair dyes, and plastic surgeons.

Even though our bodies change, God does not. He is the same yesterday, now, and forever. It is such a comfort to know that even though we age and our bodies waste away, our God is constant. 2 Corinthians 4:16 encourages us with a very interesting perspective, though we are fading on the outside, on the inside we are continually being made new. The footnote in my Bible to this verse says we are renewed daily by the "inextinguishable flame of the resurrection life of Jesus burning within." We are ignited with the Holy Spirit, don't you just love that? He's our pilot light.

As we progress in life and get *long in the tooth,* I want to always remember what the verse in Proverbs 16:31 says, "The silver-haired head is a crown of glory, if it is found in the way of righteousness."(NKJV) So, what is being said is the gray hair signifies wisdom which has been earned through the aging process.

"But grow in the grace and knowledge of our Lord and Savior Jesus Christ. To him be glory both now and forever! Amen."

2 Peter 3:18

GROWING LIKE A WEED

Usually when someone says you're *growing like a weed,* they're **talking** to a child about how fast they're growing because weeds typically grow faster than flowers. Grandma said this all the time to her grandbabies.

I love to garden; I get it honest because Mama loved to play in the dirt too. I enjoy planting flowers, especially ones which attract butterflies and bees. Regardless of what I plant, the weeds always seem to grow faster.

Our lives are much like a garden. The seeds we plant grow in our heart. When we focus on biblical truths, we produce the fruit of the Spirit, however when we harbor anger, resentment, envy, or other negative characteristics, they keep us from growing toward spiritual maturity.

When we become Christians, we begin a relationship with Jesus and the Holy Spirit empowers us to grow in our faith. We are called to grow in spiritual wisdom and understanding so we can reflect the love of God to those around us.

Through God's Word, we gain an understanding which penetrates our hearts to change us. Paul writes to the church of Colosse to make sure the people understand the difference between knowing biblical facts and having biblical knowledge; which is wisdom and understanding resulting in a life reflecting His attributes. The difference is applying what we learn and implementing it in our lifestyle. If we're not growing in our walk with the Lord, we are stagnant.

The Lord desires our faith to *grow like a weed* when we become believers. Colossians 1:10 reveals what happens when we grow in His grace, saying, "And we pray this in order that you may live a life worthy of the Lord and may please him in every way: bearing fruit in every good work, growing in the knowledge of God,".

> *"Cast all your anxiety on him because he cares for you."*
>
> 1 Peter 5:7

A STONE'S THROW

The idiom *a stone's throw* comes from the scripture Luke 22:41 where Jesus speaks of the distance a stone can be tossed, "He withdrew about a stone's throw beyond them, knelt down and prayed,".

My grandma's house sat on a ten acre hill. Three of her children ended up living right on the property after they married while our family lived a whole three miles away. Family get-togethers were often because most lived only a *stone's throw away*. My cousins were my first friends, and it was wonderful growing up with them so close, our love for one another was unquestionable.

One of the first lessons I learned as a new believer was that Jesus carries the burdens for us. We're not alone. It's a very common imagery for us to lay our burdens at the foot of the cross. I picture this as a very tender moment.

In 1 Peter chapter 5, apostle Peter writes to the elders giving them clear instructions on how to live a life full of grace. As elders in the church, they were called to live to a higher standard and set the example of Christ. He tells them in 1 Peter 5:7 to, "Cast all your anxiety on him because he cares for you." To cast something is a deliberate act and usually you're aiming at a target with force.

Rather than laying down our concerns, Peter is telling us to cast our anxiety at Jesus. Whenever something is thrown at us, our instincts are to lift our arms, cup our hands, and catch. Jesus is holding His arms out ready to catch all we toss at Him. But for this to happen we have to let go and deliberately throw our cares at Him.

As much as my family loves one another, Jesus loves us even more. What a beautiful revelation to know we're cared for so much and He's never more than *a stone's throw* away, always ready to lighten our load and make the catch.

"And not only do they become idlers, but also gossips and busybodies, saying things they ought not to."

1 Timothy 5:13b

MIND YOUR OWN BEE'S WAX

Mind your own bee's wax is a funny way to remind someone to mind their own business. This phrase was coined from the use of actual wax on a lady's face to hide acne or a blemish. Ouch! The problem was when it was hot outside or they got too close to the fire, the wax on their face would melt.

There are numerous Scriptures giving us stern warnings about gossip and how destructive it can be. Grandma used to always say, "You need to clean the dirt from your own back door before you start talking about somebody else's". There's a lot of truth in that statement. We need to make a conscious decision we won't engage in a conversation not concerning us unless we're asked to pray.

We are born with an appetite for knowledge, we just want to know things. Spend time with a three-year-old and the tsunami of questions will soon ensue. As adults, we still have a thirst for knowledge, however some topics are none of our concern and we just have to leave it alone. Paul writes in 2 Thessalonians 3:11, "We hear that some among you are idle. They are not busy; they are busybodies." He is calling out those who meddle and are interfering in the business of others without merit.

Gossip can sever relationships and the Bible makes it crystal clear as Christians we can't participate. When we use our tongue in a negative way it can have devastating effects on others because instead of building them up, we're tearing them down.

Gossip is digested and stored in our hearts causing dissension among others. As believers, it's in our best interest to *mind our own bee's wax* and not ever use our tongue as a weapon towards others.

"Everyone was amazed and gave praise to God. They were filled with awe and said, We have seen remarkable things today."

Luke 5:26

COULDN'T BELIEVE MY EYES

Couldn't believe my eyes means to be surprised or totally shocked. The origin of this phrase is unclear, but it's associated with seeing something so amazing you have a difficult time believing it.

Have you ever had something happen that just blew your socks off because you never saw it coming? I remember when I turned fifty, my husband gave me a surprise birthday party. It was great because all my friends took time out of their day to make my day special.

Jesus would make everyone He met feel special. He would heal anyone getting close enough to Him so the rumors of this great healer spread. In Matthew 5, on this one particular day, friends of a paralytic carried him to meet Jesus. The crowd was so thick in the house they decided to go onto the roof and lower the man through the tiles right in front of Jesus.

I imagine the room was packed with people all trying to get up close to Jesus when all of a sudden, a commotion was coming from above. As Jesus looks up, a man is coming down on a mat. The beautiful thing about this story is the loyalty of this man's friends. They put their life on hold to carry him from who knows where so their friend could be healed. This is faith in action.

What happened next left everyone amazed. Jesus commanded the man to get up, pick up his mat and go home. Without hesitation the man stood up and left praising God. It says everyone in the presence of Jesus *couldn't believe their eyes,* and they praised God for what they had witnessed.

"My flesh and my heart may fail, but God is the strength of my heart and my portion forever."

Psalm 73:26

A SHOT IN THE ARM

The phrase *a shot in the arm* is said when someone feels invigorated or stimulated. This originated when injections were first given to inoculate us against diseases, as in vaccinations.

Mama had a friend who would periodically come by so she could get a shot of B12. She was anemic so needed the vitamin supplement to help boost her energy level. I have days when I haven't slept very well the night before and I think I could use a shot to give me a boost. I have days when I feel spiritually sluggish also. I go through the motions of doing my devotions but am I really taking the time and allowing God to speak to me and listen.

Isaiah 40:31 is one of my favorite verses, "but those who hope in the Lord will renew their strength. They will soar on wings like eagles; they will run and not grow weary; they will walk and not be faint." We had a brilliant pastor when we lived in Charlotte, and he constantly gave us the Latin or Hebrew meaning of a word in the Scriptures. The word "renew" in Hebrew when used as a verb means "change of clothes" which ties back to Romans 13:14 when Paul tells us to clothe ourselves with Christ.

When we are weak, that's when we're our strongest because His strength shines through. Hebrews 12:1 says, "Therefore, since we are surrounded by such a great cloud of witnesses, let us throw off everything that hinders and the sin that so easily entangles, and let us run with perseverance the race marked out for us." I love to read the footnotes that scholars put in my Bible to help me have a deeper understanding of God's Word. It explains the "cloud of witnesses" are the heroes of the past who inspire us to finish the race. The Christian life is a long-distance marathon rather than a sprint, so we need strength to endure.

"I will be like the dew to Israel; he will blossom like a lily."

Hosea 14:5a

BLOOM WHERE YOU'RE PLANTED

The idiom *bloom where you're planted* means to make the best of every circumstance you find yourself in. It's all about our attitude and outlook on life.

When we were first married, we lived in a very quaint small town in South Carolina. One of my friends there was having a hard time adjusting to the area. She was a recent transplant with a new baby and only renting their home. She wanted to fix it up but didn't want to throw money away either. I encouraged her to "bloom where she was planted" and do little things to make that house her home. When we feel good about ourselves others want to be around us.

God wants us to flourish so we can continue to grow stronger in our faith. In Jeremiah 17:7-8, God reminds us when we keep our confidence in the Lord, we will be like a tree planted by the water's edge, the leaves will always be green because there is a constant source of nourishment for its roots.

Isn't that a beautiful analogy of how we're to live our life? When we stay rooted in Him, we will never wither and we're able to bear fruit. The surrounding conditions don't affect us because our hope comes from the Lord, not from outside influences. As our faith flourishes, God enables us to show others His goodness through us.

Whether we have been planted in the same place for years or we're a recent transplant to a new area, God wants us to *bloom where you're planted* and praise Him for what He has blessed us with. He loves us so much and wants us to stay rooted in the living water.

> "Whatever you do, work at it with all your heart, as working for the Lord, not for men,"
>
> Colossians 3:23

'FAIR TO MIDDLIN

If you ask someone how they're doing and their reply is, "Oh, *fair to middlin*", they're doing slightly better than average. The phrase originated from the grading system of farmer's raw cotton when it was taken to market.

God loves His people, no question about it. He wants us to live an abundant life serving in love and deeds and He doesn't want us to take our relationship with Him for granted.

God sent Amos to tell Israel and the surrounding nations He was going to send judgment on them for their immorality and sinful nature if they didn't repent. During this time great prosperity was enjoyed, while being faithful to God's commandments was forgotten. Corruption was sweeping the land. God was sad at the state of the nation because He was no longer the focus of the people. It sounds familiar, doesn't it?

Thankfully we can put our trust in the Lord and not those around us. God created us in His image and desires for us to continually grow in His likeness, refining us as we grow more dependent on Him. He doesn't want us to live in mediocrity but have a zealousness for the life we've been given.

Revelation 3:16 gives us a stern warning about not being committed in our faith, it says, "So, because you are lukewarm—neither hot nor cold—I am about to spit you out of my mouth." I don't think that could be any clearer. We can't profess to believe if we have one foot in the darkness because *fair to middlin'*, is unacceptable to God.

"Come to me, all you who are weary and burdened, and I will give you rest."

Matthew 11:28

RODE HARD AND PUT UP WET

If someone refers to someone or something being *rode hard and put up wet*, they're saying they look exhausted and worn out. This is an old saying referring to a horse being ridden until it breaks into a sweat and is put into a stall without being dried off.

As a new Christian, I needed a Bible I could understand when I read it. Our pastor at the time suggested I get the New International Version Study Bible because it has notes to enhance study time, so in 1989 my husband gave me one for my birthday.

To say my Bible looks worn is an understatement. I have highlighted, underlined, written in the margin, folded, and even spilled coffee in it a time or two. I cherish this book because the words have guided, taught, instructed, and comforted me through the years.

Hebrews 4:12 says, "For the word of God is alive and active. Sharper than any double-edged sword, it penetrates even to dividing soul and spirit, joints and marrow; it judges the thoughts and attitudes of the heart." This book is written to reveal God's love for us, and the quest Jesus has to reunite us with our Heavenly Father.

What a comfort to know when we're down, distraught, disheveled, disheartened, or discouraged, we can go to the living Word of God and seek refuge. Jesus is often referred to as the light. When it's dark, we stumble and trip but when our path is illuminated, we can see where to step. The same principle applies to God's Word because as we submerge ourselves in the Scriptures, we begin to manifest the attributes of Christ, reflecting His goodness. He is able to show us the way and keep us on our feet.

As I look at the wrinkled, battered and worn pages of my Bible, I'm thankful for the evidence it's been *rode hard and put up wet* because I've chosen not to do this life on my own.

"Let us hold unswervingly to the hope we profess, for he who promised is faithful."

Hebrews 10:23

GET A GRIP

I find it interesting to investigate the origins of idioms and see how some of the meanings have evolved through the years. *Get a grip* comes from the amount of cash which would fit between a hustler's index finger and thumb. Today when it's used, it simply means to calm down and not lose control.

My girlfriend was telling me about their experience while moving their daughter into an apartment. While pulling a trailer up a mountainous road, the trailer and truck started sliding backwards. The combination of the steep grade, heavy load and worn tires caused them to lose traction and slide out of control. Fortunately, they were able to regain control and navigate to safety, but it was scary to say the least.

Isn't life like that sometimes? We're going into certain situations blindly thinking, "I've got this!" Then around the next corner is an unexpected blow and we just wonder how much more we can take. It's a challenge to stay in control.

Even the disciples had a hard time keeping it together. When Jesus was being arrested in Gethsemane, Peter was so angry he lost control and cut the right ear off the high priest servant with a sword.

Paul writes in Galatians 5:22-23, "But the fruit of the Spirit is love, joy, peace, patience, kindness, goodness, faithfulness, gentleness, and self-control." He lists nine virtuous characteristics produced by the Holy Spirit living in the Christian but uses the comparison to the singular fruit. One single fruit produces all these virtues.

The process of obtaining all these virtuous qualities is a journey of submitting to the Lord. Through prayer and supplication, we are given the ability to *get a grip* and know we have the Holy Spirit to help us keep it together.

"Even a fool is thought wise if they keep silent, and discerning if he holds his tongue."

Proverbs 17:28

WISE AS AN OWL

To say anyone is *as wise as an owl* means they have sound judgment, are intelligent, and discerning. The owl is associated with wisdom because he looks so pensive and scholarly. This can actually be traced back to Ancient Greece where he was the symbol for the goddess of wisdom, Athena.

Mama had a friend who kept a dictionary on her kitchen table so she could learn the definition and spelling of a new word every day. She believed knowledge was powerful and said the day you stop learning is the day you die.

If you ask anyone who the wisest person in the Old Testament is, the answer would be Solomon. In the first 11 chapters of 1 Kings, we learn about the life of Solomon. When he first reigned over Israel, God told him he would give him anything. All Solomon asked for was godly wisdom.

In this day and age, it's especially important as believers we use good judgment and sift through all the information we're inundated with. We're called to test what we're being told against God's Word. In chemistry, a litmus test is performed to test the acidity of a substance, but we too have to test the validity of a statement to make sure it's biblical. Just because someone says it to be true, doesn't mean it's true.

Ephesians 4:14 warns us about distorted teachings when we aren't discerning, "Then we will no longer be infants, tossed back and forth by the waves, and blown here and there by every wind of teaching and by the cunning and craftiness of men in their deceitful scheming." This is an imagery showing the instability of those who are not strong Christians and how easily they can be swayed into other religions. We have to be moored to God, otherwise we just go whichever-way the wind blows.

The best way for us to become a discerning Christian is to read and study the Scriptures. This helps develop a relationship with Christ so we can be as *wise as an owl,* grounded in biblical truths and constantly seeking godly wisdom.

"Create in me a pure heart, O God, and renew a steadfast spirit within me."

Psalm 51:10

PURE AS THE DRIVEN SNOW

To be *as pure as the driven snow* means to be completely flawless, absolutely innocent and virtuous. This idiom comes from the fact that during a snowstorm, the wind creates drifts of snow which are untainted and clean.

There's nothing like holding a newborn baby! Their skin is as smooth as silk and they're morally perfect. There's just something so special about the miracle of birth. The intricate details have all been perfectly knitted together to create this tiny human.

We come into this world kicking and screaming. We are pushed out of our warm cozy comfort zone on day one and into a cold bright world. The instincts we're born with kick in and we begin to search for nourishment. This is a huge transition for us as we thrive to survive.

As we grow and begin to develop our personalities, it doesn't take long for our sin nature to start rearing its head. We're no longer the compliant child who is agreeable to everything, but we become defiant when we don't get our way and throw a temper tantrum.

The possibility of us remaining perfect is impossible! We can thank our sister Eve for enticing Adam to take a bite of that fruit. It's called free will. God gave them a choice and they blew it. That's when sin entered the world and it's been an uphill battle ever since. Although we can never be perfect, we can strive to have a pure heart.

The word pure means not mixed with other substances lowering the quality. It is uncontaminated. That is exactly what God has called us to be… pure. We can't allow outside influences and distractions to contaminate our relationship with God. He wants all of us and wants us to continually choose Him.

Every time we get a huge snowfall, everything as far as you can see is covered in a blanket of snow. The only sounds you hear are the branches brushing against one another as they wrestle with the wind. As I look at this beauty, I can't help but see the purity of God. An unblemished landscape.

We will never be as *pure as the driven snow,* but we can make a conscious decision to really make an effort to put God first in our lives. The only way to do this is to study God's Word so it will penetrate our heart.

"Be completely humble and gentle; be patient, bearing with one another in love."

Ephesians 4:2

HAVING ONE GOAT DOESN'T MAKE YOU A FARMER'

When anyone says to another person, *having one goat doesn't make you a farmer,* they're reminding them they're being a know-it-all, arrogant, or prideful.

Arrogance and pride are two-character traits not talked about favorably in the Scriptures. The Greek meaning of the word arrogance is "puffing up the soul". In 1 Corinthians 8:1, Paul says, "We know that we all possess knowledge. Knowledge puffs up, but love builds up." God is reminding us we can't let our wisdom fill us with pride.

When we lived in Charlotte, one of the top TV evangelists lived near us. When he first started his ministry, I think his heart may have been in the right place but as his bank account grew so did his pride. He got so "puffed up" he lost his vision and forgot who he was serving.

We're supposed to be humble. When we allow pride to become dominant in our lives, we're not giving God the glory. Numerous times in the Old Testament we see kings like Hezekiah and Ahaz, who gained power and then would flaunt their arrogance because they were so proud of their own accomplishments. Their arrogance ultimately led to failed monarchies.

God wants us to remember when we are in conversations with others to remain humble and be a better listener. We don't need to brag or be boastful because we know everything we have is a gift from the Lord. Without His grace and blessings, we are nothing and just because we have *one goat doesn't make us a farmer.*

> "Be self-controlled and alert. Your enemy the devil prowls around like a roaring lion looking for someone to devour."
>
> 1 Peter 5:8

A WOLF IN SHEEP'S CLOTHING

A wolf in sheep's clothing actually originated from Matthew 7:15 where Jesus warns us saying, "Watch out for false prophets. They come to you in sheep's clothing, but inwardly they are ferocious wolves." This idiom can be applied to anyone who is deceiving and not who they say they are.

When we first moved to Virginia one of our first priorities was to find a church home. We knew we wanted a church where the Scripture was taught, and the love of Jesus was felt.

As the body of Christ, we're called to test what we're being taught against the Word of God. Biblical truth is imperative to have a relationship with Jesus. Paul was concerned for the welfare of the churches because they were being persecuted and didn't want them to become "watered down". Many of the New Testament letters were written to the new believers about false teachings and the importance of staying true to the gospel of Jesus Christ.

As our relationship with Jesus grows, so does our biblical knowledge. God instills in us a hunger to learn and seek the truth. But we still have to remain vigilant and test what is being said against the Scriptures. Just because it's said from a pulpit, doesn't mean it's a biblically sound truth. The truth will never contradict itself.

We have to make sure what we hear is coming from the Scriptures and are not twisted words telling us what we want to hear. Let's face it, the truth hurts sometimes but when it's taught in love rather than condemnation, we hear what is said and start to turn from our sinful ways. That's when real growth starts to happen.

With the power of the Holy Spirit, we are given discernment so we're not gullible and don't believe everything we hear. We now have the boldness to stand up for the truth and call out *the wolf in sheep's clothing.*

"Then will the eyes of the blind be opened and the ears of the deaf unstopped."

Isaiah 35:5

DEAF IN ONE EAR AND CAN'T HEAR OUT OF THE OTHER

If someone is hard of hearing, another person trying to be funny might tell them they're *deaf in one ear and can't hear out of the other.* Having hearing loss is no laughing matter. It can lead to isolation, depression, and leave a person frustrated. It's important to be sensitive to those around us who have hearing loss.

Mama had significant hearing loss, so she wore hearing aids. One night while watching a sitcom, Daddy gradually turned down the volume on the television. As she keeps adjusting her hearing aids and checking the batteries, he's pretending to kill himself laughing at the program. She's becoming more and more frustrated because she's missing out on the fun. Needless to say, once she caught on, she wasn't too happy with him.

In Isaiah 35, he's speaking about a different kind of deafness. He's talking about being spiritually deaf, someone who has heard the plan of salvation, but has rejected it. A person whose heart has become hardened and wants nothing to do with God.

Isaiah 35:4 reminds us of Jesus's return, "Be strong, do not fear; your God will come, he will come with vengeance; with divine retribution he will save you." In the end, all will hear, and all will see the glory of God, but it may be too late for some. As a believer, it's imperative to share the gospel with others.

For the ones we love who are spiritually *deaf in one ear and can't hear out of the other,* we need to continue to pray for their ears to be unstopped. Don't give up hope because God loves them and longs for them to become part of the flock. He encourages us to keep showing love and being a reflection of Jesus.

> "Sing to the Lord a new song, for he has done marvelous things; his right hand and his holy arm have worked salvation for him."
>
> Psalm 98:1

COST AN ARM AND A LEG

When anyone says it's going to *cost an arm and a leg,* it's an exaggeration of how expensive something is. There are a couple of theories of where this originated, one being it was more expensive for a portrait to include arms and legs in the painting and the other being the human loss of limbs during war.

Sometimes the cost of something is greater than what we have the funds for. Jesus talks about this very thing in Luke 14:28-30, he says, when we're preparing to build something, we must first lay out the cost so we can know if we have enough money to complete the project.

When Jesus was recruiting the disciples, He laid out the exact price it would cost, they had to be willing to drop everything, pick up His cross and follow. Luke 14:33 says, "any of you who does not give up everything he has cannot be my disciple." Jesus did not mince words in this statement, He wanted people who were all in and dedicated to the call.

I have tried to imagine how it was when these men were approached by Jesus in the midst of going about their day. James and John literally dropped their nets and left their father in the boat without reservation to follow Jesus. I've asked myself, "Would I be willing to leave my family, pick up, and go?" I can't honestly answer that question, but the Scriptures say we'll never be asked to do something we're not equipped to do.

Regardless of where we are in our life, Jesus is calling us to follow Him. It *cost Him more than an arm and a leg* to bring us salvation, it cost everything. God's love for us was so deep He sent Jesus to go through an agonizing death so we can have eternal life with our Heavenly Father. Now we have the choice to put God first in our life and pleasing Him should be our number one priority.

ACKNOWLEDGMENTS

To say writing a book is a journey is an understatement. First and foremost, I have to thank the Lord who has encouraged, directed, and motivated me through this entire process. I have definitely felt His presence as He laid on my heart what to write when connecting these idioms with Scriptures.

I can't thank my husband enough for his unconditional love, support, and encouragement given to me every step of the way. I love you more each day.

I have been overwhelmed by the unwavering love and support I have received from my four children; Morgan, Tyler, Hailey, and Sydney who helped launch this entire voyage when they asked me to write down the quirky phrases they grew up hearing. You are my world and I love you all dearly, thank you!

I am so grateful to my sister-in-law, Nancy Horsley who graciously devoted time editing my manuscript. She is so incredibly talented and insightful which gave fresh eyes to reveal my oversights and blunders. I am blessed to have you as a friend.

I have to give a heartfelt thank you to my two wonderful sisters in Christ; Laura Byers and LoJuanna Pages who have endorsed, inspired, and critiqued my work. You both propel me to be a better person every day.

I can't say enough about my parents and Grandma Thomas who loved me unconditionally and molded me into the person I am today. Growing up in the South, these idioms were woven into the fiber of my being because I heard them every day.

I want to say thank you to my wonderful Uncle Dave and Aunt Linda Schuchard who radiate the love of Jesus and have graciously showered that love on me my entire life. I love you both.

REFERENCES

Carle, E. (2008). The grouchy ladybug. Modan Publishing House Ltd.

Carty, Joyce Carolyn (n.d.) Footprints in the Sand Retrieved August 29, 2022 from https://www.goodreads.com/book/show/6455467-footprints-in-the-sand

Martin, G. (n.d.). Phrases, sayings and proverbs we use everyday - with their meanings and origins explained. Phrasefinder. Retrieved August 19, 2022, from https://www.phrases.org.uk/

Oxford Learner's dictionaries: Find definitions, translations, and grammar explanations at Oxford Learner's dictionaries. Oxford Learner's Dictionaries | Find definitions, translations, and grammar explanations at Oxford Learner's Dictionaries. (2022). Retrieved August 19, 2022, from https://www.oxfordlearnersdictionaries.com/us/

Pollard, A. Adelaide (1906) Have Thine Own Way, Lord Retrieved August 29, 2022, from https//library.timelesstruths.org/music/Have_Thine_Own_Way_Lord/

Theidioms.com. Idioms. (2022). Retrieved August 19, 2022, from https://www.theidioms.com/

T. Nelson Publishers. (1992). Nkjv exhaustive concordance: New king James Version

Zondervan Corporation. (1985). The Niv Study Bible.

All the photography in this book was taken by Kim Johnson.

ABOUT THE AUTHOR

Hi! My name is Kimberly Johnson. I am a wife, mother of four, Mimmy, sister, and friend. I enjoy hiking, chasing sunsets, spending time with grandchildren, and camping.

My husband and I have lived in Christiansburg, Virginia for the past 26 years where I continue to dig deeper into God's word through Bible studies. I am a novice when it comes to writing but creating this book has been exhilarating.

I'm from North Carolina where I grew up hearing idioms from my parents and grandma. My grandma was influential in my life so many of the stories are straight from her.

My children encouraged me to write down the sayings they in turn heard when they were growing up and the Lord laid on my heart to turn them into devotions.

I have a blog khj4761.wixsite.com/bloomingwithjesus and I'm on Instagram @blooming.with.jesus

CPSIA information can be obtained
at www.ICGtesting.com
Printed in the USA
JSHW050949030323
38388JS00007B/19